HOW TO HELP YOUR GIFTED CHILD

A HANDBOOK FOR PARENTS AND TEACHERS

The Gifted Child Society, Inc.

GINA GINSBERG AND
CHARLES H. HARRISON

MONARCH PRESS

Dedication

This book is dedicated to all parents and teachers whose children do things a little earlier, a little better, a little faster, and—maybe—a little differently from most other children.

Acknowledgments

The Gifted Child Society gratefully acknowledges the grant from the Ford Foundation and the cooperation of the many parents and educators which made this book possible.

Published by
MONARCH PRESS
A Simon & Schuster Division of
Gulf & Western Corporation
Simon & Schuster Building
1230 Avenue of the Americas
New York, N.Y. 10020

ISBN: 0-671-18759-7

Printed in the United States of America

CONTENTS

Foreword v

Introduction vii

Part I For Parents of Gifted Children

Chapter 1 Is Your Child Gifted? 1

Chapter 2 What Help Can You Expect from Your Child's School? 9

Chapter 3 You're Not Alone 17

Chapter 4 You Need to Organize 21

Chapter 5 By-Laws and All That Jazz 30

Chapter 6 Workers Needed 34

Chapter 7 If Money Doesn't Grow on Trees, Where Does It Come From? 50

Chapter 8 Keeping Track of the Money 55

Chapter 9 Choosing a Format for the Educational Program 60

Chapter 10 Which Children Should Be Admitted? 66

Chapter 11 Deciding What Courses to Offer 72

Chapter 12 Finding, Guiding, and Keeping the Right Teachers 84

Chapter 13 Scheduling Teachers and Learning 96

Chapter 14 Publicize What You're Doing 108

Chapter 15 Winning Friends and Influencing People 118

Part II For Teachers of Gifted Children

Chapter 16 Characteristics of the Gifted Child   125

Chapter 17 Establishing Goals for You and Your Students   127

Chapter 18 Preparing to Teach   132

Chapter 19 Techniques for Teaching That Really Work   158

Chapter 20 Materials That Can Help   161

Chapter 21 Tapping the Community and Parents   164

Chapter 22 What You Need to Know   166

Afterword   171

Appendix A — Gifted Child Society Constitution and By-Laws   173

Appendix B — Job Descriptions   181

Appendix C — Letter and Questionnaire   185

Appendix C — Letter and Questionnaire   185

Appendix D — The Saturday Workshops   188

Appendix E — A Typical Advertisement   195

Appendix F — A Letter in Support of Bill S-874   197

FOREWORD

It has been said with considerable justification that gifted children are the most disadvantaged of our school population. One has only to survey the variety of programs for exceptional children mandated in most states to see how low a priority is assigned to special programs for the gifted.

Thus, we find in almost all states special provisions for the mentally retarded, the physically handicapped, children with learning disabilities, and non-English speaking children, but far less than half the states concern themselves with the gifted.

We mouth the clichés and give lip service to the ideal that the goal of education is to help children reach their potential. In practice, schools are more concerned with helping children reach the so-called "norm" of achievement than with developing potential, and they become too easily satisfied and delighted with children who function merely at, or above grade level. This misinterpretation of the purpose of the school is reenforced by our current philosophy of egalitarianism with its aim of equal education for all, and its resulting acceptance of mediocrity.

Equal education, however, is not the same as equal opportunity—opportunity to receive the best and most *appropriate* education tailored to meet special individual needs. Contrary to popular opinion, intellectual and creative ability cannot survive educational neglect, and where there is no special provision for the gifted, these children with the greatest potential rarely are identified, and even less often do they perform on a level consistent with their abilities. To this extent, they are the most disadvantaged segment of our school population.

A recent twenty-year study of black and white children which followed them from kindergarten through high school and beyond, clearly showed that where a school program provided no opportunities for children to display their gifts and talents, such gifts and talents were never exhibited. Conversely, where the special needs of gifted children were recognized and programs were provided, children were discovered who could paint, sing, act, or dance, or who could grapple with complex intellectual problems.

It is a misconception in American life to believe that educational programs originate exclusively in professional circles. One can make a long list of recent special programs which have been a direct result of court decisions or legislative action, preceded in almost every case by parental concern and militancy.

This book is a fascinating account not only of parental organization on behalf of the gifted but also of the establishment of an extensive enrichment program not offered by the schools. The authors have been deeply involved with the program since its inception, and Mrs. Ginsberg's enthusiasm and dedication comes through clearly. The step-by-step approach in enlisting parental interest, obtaining school cooperation, and generating legislative activity can serve as a blueprint for parents of gifted and talented children.

PHILIP E. KRAUS
Professor of Education
Hunter College of the City University of New York

INTRODUCTION

In 1958 Mrs. Marshall W. Lynn resigned from the Gifted Child Society of New Jersey. So, big deal!

In a way it was a big deal. Mrs. Lynn's resignation was a symbol of those conditions that cause parents of gifted children everywhere to search outside the public schools for ways to enrich the lives of their children.

Mrs. Lynn, one of the founders of the Gifted Child Society in 1957, was unlike the other organizers. She was not the parent of a gifted child but a high school math teacher. Her concern was for all the above-average children who were receiving an average education. When Mrs. Lynn joined the Society, it was still a study group examining the characteristics and needs of gifted children. But it wasn't long before the parents in the organization began to develop an out-of-school program designed to meet the needs identified earlier by their research. Reports of the Society's activities soon appeared in local newspapers — not under big headlines on page one, but under small headlines on back pages, the pages read by Mrs. Lynn's high school principal. He called her into his office one day. In a tone reserved for solemn occasions he suggested that community residents might get the impression that she catered more to bright children than to not-so-bright children. Mrs. Lynn took the hint. At the next meeting of the Society she handed in her resignation.

But the Society refused to quit. It never believed the implication that special treatment of the most able might somehow be a denial of the assertion in the Declaration of Independence that all men are created equal. And it never believed that bright children are bright enough to teach themselves if classroom instruction bores them.

Precisely because the Society's parents *didn't* butt out and let the schools determine what was best and sufficient for the children the Gifted Child Society grew to become one of the nation's largest nonprofit, parent-run organizations. It offers gifted children out-of-school enrichment while it continues to hope and work for the day when the

vii

public schools will do what is best and sufficient for the very bright and very talented. Today, the Gifted Child Society offers several dozen courses to more than 500 children from northern New Jersey and southern New York each fall and spring in Saturday workshops and a summer session. More than 10,000 children have participated so far.

About a dozen years after Mrs. Lynn resigned from the Gifted Child Society, the U.S. Department of Health, Education and Welfare invited representatives of the Society to testify before a panel gathering information for a report that the U.S. Commissioner of Education was to issue to the Congress on the state of education for the gifted and talented in America. That was December 1970. The subsequent report of the commissioner, which is now starting to prompt state and federal governments and the nation's schools to design and finance new programs for the gifted and talented, showed that the Society may have been wise all along.

In answering the question, "Aren't special provisions undemcratic?" Commissioner S.P. Marland, Jr., replied: "If we believe that democratic education means appropriate educational opportunities and the right to education in keeping with one's ability to benefit, the answer is no. Rather than argue that special planning is undemocratic, one might conclude that the special planning should be carried on for the benefit of democracy."

The commissioner's report concluded: "There is an enormous individual and social cost when talent among the nation's children and youth goes undiscovered and undeveloped. These students cannot ordinarily excel without assistance." And in response to those who argue that the public schools should be allowed to do their job without outside interference or outside help, the report stated: "Identification of the gifted is hampered ... by apathy and even hostility among teachers, administrators, guidance counselors, and psychologists. Differentiated education for the gifted and talented is presently perceived as a very low priority at federal, state, and most local levels of government and educational administration."

One of the immediate outcomes of the commissioner's report to Congress was the creation of an Office of Education of the Gifted and Talented within the U.S. Office of Education. It was that office which encouraged the Gifted Child Society to produce a handbook offering guidance both to parents and teachers of gifted children based on the Society's nearly two decades of experience. The Society might not have been wise enough to take a hint in 1958 and fade away, but it was wise enough to accept the encouragement of the U.S. Office of Education of the Gifted and Talented. This book is proof of that acceptance.

This book is the Society's attempt to help other parents of gifted children first to understand and cope with their children, and second, to organize for the dual purposes of urging the public schools to offer more and better learning opportunities for gifted children and for actually providing enrichment when the schools can't or won't. Instead of drowning parents in a sea of theories and bibliographies, the Society hopes to give them a chance to swim on their own by telling them what the Society has discovered about gifted children: what gifted children think and feel, what they want and need, what the Society has learned — its successes and failures through the years, as it designed, implemented and evaluated a constantly changing and expanding program for children aged four to early teens. The book also offers the experience and acquired knowledge of the Society's teachers to other teachers and would-be teachers of the gifted.

• Instead of reporting what university scholars say are early signs of gitedness in children, this book reports what actually has tipped off parents of gifted children.

• Instead of describing in general terms how to put together an organization of parents that can last two decades and then some, this book offers the fundamentals: what should and should not go into the by-laws, what officers and committees are needed, and what they should do. It tells how to set up financial records that efficiently keep track of the dollars and cents.

• Instead of talking about hiring teachers in the abstract, this book talks about what Society parents have looked for in prospective teachers and what they have found, and how their choices have worked out or have not worked out in the classroom.

• Instead of discoursing on general learning theories, this book reports what teaching techniques have actually worked in the classroom and what kinds of learning experiences have proved beneficial to gifted and talented children.

Part I

FOR PARENTS OF GIFTED CHILDREN

Chapter 1

Is Your Child Gifted?

Many books have been written defining giftedness and cataloguing its outward characteristics. We do not propose to devote our book to the subject; we have neither the desire nor the competence to write a scholarly tract. While we will refer to some experts' testimony, mostly we will offer the findings and observations accumulated over the years by the parents and teachers of the Gifted Child Society. We do not think it an idle boast to call it wisdom.

What Does It Mean to Be Gifted?

The report of the U.S. Commissioner of Education to the Congress in 1971 pretty much defined giftedness this way: Gifted children are those children who consistently perform, or are capable of performing, at a very high level. In addition, the high level at any given stage of the child's life is considerably beyond the level normally expected of a child at that age.

Dr. Wm. Wendell Williams, president of the Gifted Child Society in the early 1960s and a professional educator, warns that some children can score all A's in their courses and still not be gifted. The child simply may do very well with the amount of learning required of a person of his age and grade in school.

1

Signs to Look for in Your Child

Not all parents know instinctively whether or not their children are gifted. In fact, there are more parents who have gifted children and don't know it than there are parents who don't have gifted children but think they do. The Society has been pleasantly surprised over the years to discover that officers' phones and mailboxes are not perpetually deluged with inquiries or demands from parents who mistakenly think their children are gifted. It is a myth that most parents think their children are geniuses.

The U.S. Commissioner of Education, in his report to Congress, said one of the best summaries of traits in the gifted was devised by Catherine Cox Miles, who studied the childhood of 100 geniuses. Here are the important characteristics she listed: independence of thought, perceptiveness, understanding, trustworthiness, conscientiousness, strength of influence on others, persistence, devotion to distant goals, and a desire to excel.

The Connecticut State Department of Education, in advising parents of characteristics of gifted children, offered this list: a longer attention span than normal for the child's age, a persistent curiosity, a desire to learn rapidly, a good memory, an awareness and appreciation of people and things, a wide range of interests, an ability to solve problems, and a tendency to prefer the companionship of older children or adults.

Parents of children in the Gifted Child Society's enrichment program were asked about the early evidence that made them think or convinced them that they had a gifted child. Their responses corroborated the observations of the experts, but they also made some additions to the lists and emphasized that all gifted children don't necessarily demonstrate the same characteristics.

Among the Society's parents there was a concensus that their gifted children started to do almost everything earlier than other children their age. They tended to speak earlier, read earlier, and ask more questions — more logical and searching questions — earlier. But some parents said their children were not very verbal. One mother reported that while her son didn't use words very early to express himself, he did invent a language of sounds to communicate. It took her a while to break the code. A mother whose child was very verbal at an early age said she was tipped off to his difference, if not his giftedness, by the fact that she "could talk to him like a person" at about age two.

What the experts don't tell you, but some mothers of gifted children do, is that gifted children can sometimes be a pain in the neck. They can especially bug you with a lot of questions and can run you ragged trying to keep up with them and their above average intellectual pace. We're not saying that the gifted child is wrong for asking, asking, asking or resenting the blockage of his intellectual pursuits; we're just saying that it sometimes takes a great deal of patience and unusual understanding on the part of parents to recognize some of the signs of giftedness and appreciate them.

Testing Your Child's IQ

Suppose you have observed in your child some or all of the characteristics discussed and think he is gifted, but so far your child's school has not confirmed your belief. It's possible that even if your child has been given a group IQ test the score he received does not indicate his giftedness. Group IQ tests tend to miss many gifted children (see Chapter 2). The best method for testing your child's IQ is to have him individually tested by a qualified psychologist. The tests most often administered are the Stanford-Binet intelligence tests and the Wechsler Intelligence Scale for Children.

What IQ score denotes giftedness? Most educators accept an IQ of 130 as confirmation of giftedness. However, many experts believe that most children with an IQ of at least 120 need and can benefit from an enrichment program designed for gifted children. "At a given age level one child in 1,000 would, on the average, have a Binet IQ of 148 or above and such children comprise the highly gifted group," wrote Dorothy F. Syphers in her book *Gifted and Talented Children: Practical Programing for Teachers and Principals.* The book also lists the number of children at different IQ levels that one might expect in an average population: at IQ 130, three out of 100 children; at IQ 150, one out of 1,000; at IQ 160, one out of 10,000; at IQ 168, one out of 100,000.

If you are interested in having your child individually tested and he is not yet enrolled in school, you can still go to the central school district office and ask to be referred to a psychologist or testing center. You child's pediatrician also may recommend a psychologist or clinic. The cost of individual IQ testing varies. To get good service at the lowest rate, you might sound out family or child counseling services established by local or state governments. You could also contact nearby colleges and universities. To avoid a runaround, start by asking for the institution's school or department of education. If you get nowhere there, ask for the psychology department.

If your child is already enrolled in school, you might ask the school principal or superintendent if individual testing can be arranged through the school system's psychologist or guidance center. In addition to presenting your own observations that point to giftedness in your child, you should try to provide back-up information from the child's teacher or teachers to support your request for appropriate evaluation.

What You Can Do for Your Child at Home

As a parent of a gifted child, you probably have as many questions to ask as your child does. You may wonder, for example, how you can help your gifted child without hurting the feelings of your not-so-gifted children. Should you urge your gifted child to do more studying, creating and research? Or should you be pushing him out of the house and into a gymnasium or onto a playing field so that his body won't grow weak while his mind grows strong?

Those parents who raised their first child with one hand held tightly to Dr. Spock's book remember that Dr. Spock was most valuable because his words tended to calm the panicky parent. The mother who thought a rash might be scarlet fever learned from Dr. Spock that it was probably roseola. Problems that seemed very large and peculiar only to her child turned out to be universal.

We think we can be of special help to parents of gifted children by offering them the kinds of simple tips that dispel panic, suggest behavior that they might not have considered, and reinforce what they are already doing. These tips have been gleaned from parents over the years. The fact that they also generally agree with the advice of scholars is a welcome but not unexpected coincidence.

Tip 1

Remember, we are talking about a child who also happens to be gifted. Just because a child's mental abilities may be far beyond those of children the same age, he is still going to behave like other children in most respects. Don't be surprised or annoyed when your child cries about things other children cry about. And he may sometimes throw a tantrum because he's a child. Don't expect every statement to be profound, every question to be intellectually perceptive. The gifted child also says childlike things and asks childlike questions. And the gifted child needs the same kind of parental love and guidance all children need.

Tip 2

Enjoy your gifted child because he's unique. And enjoy his brothers and sisters because they're unique in their ways. It is not necessary to concentrate a great deal more on the gifted child in order to fulfill his needs. Occasionally, he will require more time and attention, but on occasion a brother or sister will also require more time and attention — perhaps for different reasons. Don't compare the gifted child with his brothers and sisters, or vice versa. No one gains from such comparisons and everybody runs the risk of losing something — especially his individuality.

Tip 3

Don't compare your gifted child to other children in the neighborhood. Don't brag about your gifted child's exploits in front of friends and acquaintances, especially if you want to keep them as friends and acquaintances. You may do a little bragging before his grandparents, but even relatives tire of a steady recitation of how bright their grandchild/nephew/cousin is.

Tip 4

Listen to your gifted child and respond to his questions. We've already said that gifted children ask more thoughtful questions more often and at an earlier age than most other children. You may not have answers for some of the questions. In such cases, the best thing to do is to admit that you don't know and suggest other sources where the child might find the answer. With a very young child, a parent should assist him in his search. It is important to give an honest and complete answer when you can. Some children may be temporarily satisfied with such responses as "Because that's the way it is" and "It's too complicated to explain." The gifted child, however, demands a genuine answer — and most of the time he will understand it.

Tip 5

Make available to the gifted child a variety of books, magazines, newspapers, and other materials. Expose him to as many enriching experiences as possible — trips to museums, libraries, theaters, and historical sites. Give him an opportunity to meet people and to see places where he can satisfy his curiosity and challenge his intellect. One of the first things the founders of the Gifted Child Society did for their children was to arrange occassional field trips to places of interest, including companies that engaged in research or manufacture. Most of the trips your gifted child will enjoy, his brothers and sisters also will enjoy— but perhaps in a different way. If the gifted child wants to question a museum attendant about something and the other children are ready to go on to another exhibit, make arrangements to meet somewhere.

Tip 6

While providing materials and experiences, there may be a tendency to nudge or even push the gifted child in one direction or another. For example, because parents have heard that many gifted children have exceptional abilities to understand scientific concepts and theories, they may overburden and overpower their gifted child with chemistry sets and highly complex books. Don't decide the child's interests for him. He might want to explore many things simply to satisfy his curiosity and because he is capable of making the exploration.

Tip 7

If the gifted child wants to specialize in a subject, let him. The chances are there will be few opportunities during his school career to tackle a subject for as long as he wants and to turn it inside out and sideways to look at it from every angle.

Tip 8

Allow the gifted child to do for himself things he says he can do for himself. Unlike other children, the gifted child more often than not is able to measure his own capacity and ability and know his own limitations.

Tip 9

Don't overfeed your gifted child's intellectual appetite. He does not have to be engaged in some specific mental or physical activity all of the time. Give him time to stare into space and think and dream. The gifted child is a creative and inventive child, but it's hard to be creative and inventive on a full schedule of pre-planned activities.

Tip 10

All work and no play may not make Jack a dull boy, but it may make him be something he doesn't want to be. We mention again that gifted children are children first. Your gifted child may sometimes want to play baseball before or instead of working on a science project or a poem. Encourage him to play and relax, to do some things simply for the fun of it and not because they will sharpen his mind or coordinate his body. Don't force him into a sport you think would be good for him. As with all children, it must be your child's choice.

Tip 11

Praise him for his good efforts. Of course, you would do so for all your children. But the gifted child is usually taking more intellectual risks than other children, and risk taking needs to be supported. When the risks pay off, he needs commendation. And when they don't, he needs praise for trying.

Tip 12

Discipline your gifted child when he needs disciplining. Correct him when he needs correction. Give direction when he needs direction. He should not be granted special privileges nor should unacceptable behavior be tolerated because of his intellectual gifts. The gifted child should not be exempt from the rules and codes other members of the family and the community must live by.

Tip 13

Don't expect your gifted child to be gifted all of the time in all things. Tight halos give very bad headaches.

Figure 1

PROGRAMS REPORTED BY 27 MODEL DISTRICTS IN 5 STATES* WITH SUPERIOR PROGRAMS FOR CHILDREN WITH EXCEPTIONAL LEARNING NEEDS

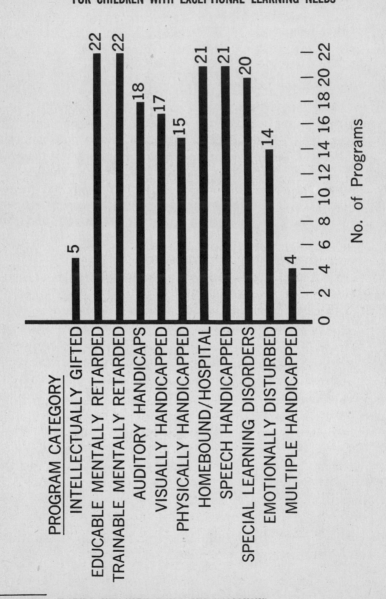

* (CALIFORNIA, FLORIDA, NEW YORK, TEXAS, AND WISCONSIN)

Source: Abstracts of National Educational Finance Project Satellite Projects Reported at First National Conference, 1970.

Chapter 2

What Help Can You Expect from Your Child's School?

What is being done for the gifted child in America's schools? In 1971, the U.S. Office of Education chose twenty-seven school systems from a national sample "because of their model programs for the children with exceptional learning needs." Then it identified the number of programs for gifted children and the number of programs for mentally and physically handicapped children. Among the twenty-seven districts, there were only five programs for the gifted. But there were a whopping 174 separate programs for children with various handicaps! (See figure 1.)

The U.S. Office of Education sent a detailed questionnaire in 1970 to 239 experts on education for the gifted in every part of the country. The experts reported "a dismal view of the adequacy of existing programs," and they concluded that "nearly all communities are described as having very few provisions, or none at all. The neglect is greatest at the early school years; but even at the secondary level, little is done. Educational planning for the gifted has had low priority, and few persons are aware of the tragic waste of human potential."

Fifty state departments of education were surveyed by the Office of Education at about the same time. "The general portrait of the state survey data is clear," said the commissioner's report. "Most of the states have recognized that the education of the gifted is an area of substantial educational need and have tried, in a variety of ways, to put some available resources to work in this area. It is also clear that these efforts have been overwhelmed by the more crisis-oriented issues of the deprived child, the disruptive child, the child who cannot learn, etc."

One of the effects of the "overwhelming" was that as of 1971 in only twenty-four states was there at least one part-time staff member charged with responsibility for programs for the gifted. And in only ten of those twenty-four states were the responsible persons able to spend more than fifty percent of their working time on programs for the gifted. "In many instances the amount of time allocated to serving gifted students is but a small fraction of a multitude of duties and responsibilities assigned to one of the high ranking state officials," said the commissioner's report.

Battling the School's Elitism Hang-up

Fred is eight years old and gifted. He is placed in the third grade along with other eight-year-olds. There may or may not be an attempt to group children by ability, but even assuming some grouping, Fred is intellectually and probably physically ahead of most or all of the children in his class. Most of the work in class is done by the class as a single group. Only occasionally is the class divided into subgroups of three, four, or five children. If the teacher isn't talking, the children probably are being questioned as a group. Fred, because of his ability, is quick to answer. And he probably provides more information than the teacher really wants (or his classmates are ready for). In a small group working on a project, Fred probably is offering ideas and elaborate plans for implementing them before some of his partners have a clear understanding of what the intent of the project is. Unless Fred stifles himself, he's probably going to get on the nerves of his teacher and the other children. By being himself, Fred may become offensive to those around him. And one definition of a snob is "a person who has an offensive air of superiority in matters of knowledge." Of course, Fred doesn't mean to be offensive. But offensiveness is sometimes in the eyes of the beholder.

Fred's mother doesn't mean to be offensive either. But she's concerned when Fred comes home day after day and tells her how bored he is and how he is put down for being first with the most. So, Fred's mother talks to the teacher or the principal or the superintendent, or all three. She only wants the school to relieve the tedium and frustration in her child's life. The teacher and principal may suspect they aren't doing all they should be doing for the child, but rather than admit it, they call the mother a snob and the child disruptive. In the eyes of the school people, Fred's mother may have gone from being concerned to being a pest and a snob even before she's aware that anybody was listening.

There's no question that some children and some parents are snobs. But most gifted children tagged with the label are victims of a bad rap. They are people exercising their differences in a climate that does not encourage or even sometimes tolerate differences.

Societal and peer pressures cause many gifted children to wish they could crawl into a corner and hide under a dunce's cap. Indeed, many teachers and parents of very bright children can recall one or more occasions when a child purposely flunked a test or failed to complete a report so he could be "just one of the gang."

A former president of the Society and a teacher of creative writing in the Society's workshops had this to say about the elitism hang-up: "Because the gifted child has ability, he is already an outsider. The kids develop cruel names for him—the 'Brain,' the 'Showoff,' etc. Emotionally he is like any other kid; he wants affection. But there is a built-in price he must pay for associating with other kids. He must pretend not to know. Also, there are teachers who say, 'Put your hand down; I know you know.' So, for hours he listens to things he already knows. He knows he's different, and he becomes a troublemaker."

Frankly, many people—including some educators—consider the gifted child and his parents to be snobs. Americans generally seem to have a knee-jerk reflex to what is, or appears to be, snobbery. They won't look up to anyone they think is looking down on them.

Many have criticized the kind of grouping that places bright children together on the grounds that it helps foster the snobbery of bright children. In reality, ability grouping can have a very humbling effect on bright children. A bright child may stand out in a class that includes children of all levels of ability. But when he is put among other bright children, he finds that he no longer stands out. He may have to stand down to even brighter children. Also, if the very bright are taken out of regular classes, other children who used to be reluctant to exercise leadership and display their ablity are now able to speak out and feel good about their ability to do so.

Of course, Americans also have an inherited fear of a ruling class. And it is this fear that raises the question that the U.S. Commissioner of Education answered only briefly in his report to Congress: "Aren't special provisions undemocratic?" Some educators are concerned that if they allow a gifted child to blaze the intellectual trails, he will go far beyond most of his classmates, that parents of other children will accuse the teacher, the principal, and others in the school system of ignoring the masses in favor of the elite. That was the charge leveled against Mrs. Lynn at the high school where she taught math. Because she recognized that gifted children need to do more and move faster than their peers, she was accused of catering to the chosen few. If we were to agree that it is undemocratic to provide special help for children of special needs, said the commissioner, "then all special educational programs would disappear, and hundreds of millions now expended by the states and the federal government would be diverted to other uses." The 174 special programs for the handicaped in the twenty-seven "model" districts would have to be scrapped. The millions spent on children with learning deficiencies under Title I of the Elementary and Secondary Education Act would have to be recalled.

One way to put down the elitism hang-up is to cite the story told by Idaho educator Janus Pierson. At a PTA meeting, Pierson moved the following proposition: (1) that the high school select the most talented boys by establishing rigorous performance tests; (2) that a talent team be formed of those boys passing the tests; (3) that high school faculty members be paid extra to teach this select group; (4) that members of the talent team wear a distinctive uniform; (5) that the boys be encouraged to compete against talented boys from other schools selected in the same fashion; and (6) that trophies and awards be created to honor the accomplishments of the talent team. Mrs. Pierson seconded the motion. In the ensuing debate, most people were critical of the plan. "Undemocratic," "expensive," "impossible," they said. "It will make snobs of our children," and "It's not fair to all children" were some of the criticisms hurled at the preposterous idea. Then Pierson stood up. "I think you ought to know," he said, "that I was not describing and proposing a new program. We have been carrying on such a program at our high school for years. We call it a football team."

Classification and Misclassification

"We just figured our son was a discipline problem," said the parents of a child in the Gifted Child Society's Saturday workshop. They had good reason to believe that he was. His first and second grade teachers told them their son was a problem—"disruptive" was the official term generally used. Their son wasn't more than two or three weeks into the third grade when his teacher called the parents and said, "How can you possibly stand him; I know I can't." The boy was sent to the psychologist, not because it was supposed that his giftedness was being frustrated but because he was being "disruptive" in class. The psychologist administered an individual IQ test and found that the child had an IQ of 154.

Among the most astounding and discouraging survey results recorded in recent years were those for the School Staffing Survey conducted by the U.S. Office of Education in 1969–1970. Almost fifty-eight percent of America's schools reported they had *no* gifted children enrolled. That's none! Zero! Not any! "The report of no gifted pupils by over half of the schools surveyed in 1969–1970 is a depressing piece of information," the Commissioner of Education reported to Congress. "The statistics may indicate widespread ignorance, apathy, and indifference, or outright hostility toward the notion that gifted and talented young people merit attention. Less effort to identify is made at the elementary level than at the secondary, although research stresses the advantages of early identification and planning. Gifted young people with the ability to invent, create, and contribute to society at an early age apparently would have little opportunity in the majority of our schools and probably no encouragement, under present conditions."

If you think your child is gifted, what are the chances that his giftedness will be confirmed by the school? Not so good, unfortunately. Most schools rely on group IQ tests and teacher observations for the determination of exceptionally bright children. Neither source is necessarily reliable. According to the U.S. Commissioner of Education, "All the study results showed that half of an identified gifted population would have remained unidentified if group tests alone had been employed. Data provided by a test publisher showed that the discrepancy between group scores and individual scores increased as the intelligence level increased. The most highly gifted children were penalized most by group test scores; that is, the higher the ability, the greater the failure of the group test to reveal such ability. Teachers are able to nominate about half of the gifted. It is unsafe to assume that teachers will identify even the highly gifted." In a study of Ohio schools in 1964, researcher Walter B. Barbe found that teachers failed to identify twenty-five percent of the most gifted children sitting in their classrooms.

If your child is Black, Puerto Rican, Indian, Mexican-American, or a member of another minority group, his chances of being identified as gifted may be somewhere between fifty-fifty and a snow-ball's chance in hell. Researcher Martin D. Jenkins analyzed data on 22,301 Black children and found that one percent had an IQ of 130 and above. Since the data were based on group IQ testing, it can be assumed that the percentage of children with an IQ above 130 was much greater.

More of the Same, or Enrichment?

Let's assume your child is gifted and everyone around him knows it—you, your child's teacher(s), and anybody else in the school system whose business it is and who is in a position to help. Let us also assume that nobody in authority, including the school board, suffers from the elitism hang-up and that there is a commitment to do *something* for gifted children. What's likely to be done?

A mother of a child in the Society's workshops once called to complain. Her child's teacher had the notion that the way to help her child was to give him one simple project after another. "He gets an A plus on a project," said the mother, "and his reward is to get another project." Often such projects are selected by the teacher to keep the gifted child occupied and quiet. The projects usually re-quire the gifted child to do more of what everybody in the class has already learned. They rarely challenge him. For example, if the class is engaged in long division, the bright child might be asked to do ten extra problems. When he gets those all right, the teacher gives him ten more, and so on.

Other than giving a gifted child projects to do and papers to write, what might teachers do? Fortunately, there are many teachers in America's public schools who recognize a superior student when they see one. They understand that he needs not only special guidance and encouragement but also latitude to explore avenues other children in his class will not travel until much later, if at all. As the commis-sioner's report indicated, there may not be enough of such teachers, but there are those who care, and even more importantly, know how to help. Indeed, there may be more such teachers than the commis-sioner's report reveals. Many teachers are strait-jacketed, like their pupils, by a system that places children of one age together in one grade. All children are expected to learn what is designed for that grade level in the same way and at the same time.

The caring, knowing teacher, if able within school regulations, will allow a gifted child to work outside the regular classroom more often than other children. This may include time in the library or the media or resource center, where the child can pursue independent research under professional guidance and encouragement. The teacher may provide opportunities for the elementary school age child to spend some time in labs and other facilities at the high school. The high school student should be given the opportunity to spend time at a nearby college or business. In class the teacher may allow the gifted child to read at his own pace and bring in additional books. The teacher may even bring in books the gifted child is likely to appreciate. The child also may work on projects largely of his own design and creation and at times when other children are engaged in repeat or review work.

There are schools where gifted children have opportunities to participate in enrichment programs at either the elementary or secondary level. Such programs are usually conducted after school or during a small portion of the regular day. If your child is enrolled in such a program, there is a simple test you might apply to find out whether it offers genuine enrichment. If your child is engaged in activities and studying subjects not otherwise possible or available to him in his regular class(es), he is probably in a true enrichment program. Another way of knowing if he's getting enrichment is to ask yourself, "Is he still tearing his hair out and causing me to do the same?"

Perhaps your gifted child is of elementary school age and enrichment for bright children does not begin in your school system until junior or senior high. Speak to the responsible school officials. Inform them that experts on gifted children almost unanimously recommend beginning enrichment programs in the early grades. Ninety-five percent of the nation's specialists in education for the gifted recommended to the U.S. Office of Education that special programs for very bright children begin at the beginning of the children's school life, but certainly by grades four or five.

Skipping Grades

Most experts on education for the gifted agree that the very bright child does not need to spend twelve years in school and four undergraduate years in college. There are reports from time to time of gifted young people skipping directly from their junior year in high school to their sophomore year in college. And there are some institutions springing up now which, in fact, combine the last two years of high school with the first two years of college. A recent report of the Carnegie Commission on Higher Education recommended such a process for a number of children in America.

While there may be merit and value to some such combination of grade levels, there may be little merit or value in merely skipping from one grade to the next. The main problem is that the gifted child is simply not so many grade levels ahead of his peers, it's that he learns differently and faster than his peers. He can handle more things at one time. He is capable of moving in directions that another grade level won't provide any more than his present grade level. As long as the school generally allows or encourages only conventional methods of learning and at only slightly varying rates, the gifted child probably will not profit from moving up from one grade to another.

Where skipping grades is practiced, girls generally benefit more than boys because girls tend to mature earlier physically. It is particularly hard on boys who are already young for their class to be moved up to another grade where there will be an even greater age gap between them and their classmates. And a boy skipped during the junior high or upper middle school years can find himself among female classmates who appear as old and as tall and grown up as the boy's Saturday night baby-sitter.

Chapter 3

You're Not Alone

You are at a PTA meeting and the speaker is describing child behavior. Parents all over the room are nodding and laughing at the same time at the same things. Most people have two reactions in such situations, suprise and relief. Parents may be suprised that so many other children behave as theirs do, but also relieved that other parents are struggling through their child's early adolescent years too. It's not just their child who turns from one emotion to another faster than he can switch from cold to hot water—they all do!

Parents of gifted children are no different. It's interesting to watch people's reactions at a meeting of parents of gifted children. One parent says she was tipped off to the fact that her child was different when he began asking so many questions so early. Parents around the room begin nodding and muttering "Uh huh." Another parent says she noticed that her daughter had a particularly keen and sophisticated sense of humor at an early age. This was an indication that she was different from some of her friends and her brother. "Yes, yes," echoes around the room.

If you're the parent of a gifted child, you have a lot of company. According to the U.S. Commissioner of Education, "a conservative estimate of the gifted and talented population ranges between 1.5 and 2.5 million children." Most people think that's *quite* conservative.

Finding Other Parents of Gifted Children

"Parents of gifted children need the support of other parents of gifted children," said one parent of a child attending the Society's Saturday workshop. But if you are in search of support—people with

17

whom you can swap observations, questions, and experiences—you'll want to conduct your search in your own neighborhood, school district, and community. How should you go about it?

Here are some possible approaches:

• Place a small ad in a local weekly or daily newspaper. Such an ad was the seed sown in the 1950s from which grew the Gifted Child Society. Recently, the mother who did most to launch the Society described how she went about it: "One day I discovered my son was not of average intelligence and ability. I was panicky. He didn't play with other children. And the questions! So, I placed an ad in the newspaper to see if other parents were in a similar situation. I received a few replies."

• If your child is in a school enrichment program, ask him for the names of some of his friends in the program. Call his friends' parents and invite them over for coffee.

• Ask your child's teacher or school principal for the names of parents of other very bright children in your child's class, grade, or school. Then follow through with phone calls and an invitation.

• If the parents' organization at your child's school publishes a newsletter, ask the editor if he or she would insert a small notice in an upcoming issue. Here are two possible versions of such a notice:

Is your child enrolled in the school's enrichment program? If so, and if you would like to talk informally with other parents of children in the program, please call Mrs.   . She is arranging a kaffee klatsch for parents.

Is your child exceptionally bright? If so, please call Mrs.   . She is arranging a kaffee klatsch for parents of exceptionally bright children.

• Instead of putting a notice in the newsletter, you might want to make an announcement at a meeting of the parents' organization.

If you don't want to be bothered with a kaffee klatsch at your home, you might arrange through the school to hold a meeting in the faculty room of the cafeteria, library, or other room after school hours. Such a meeting might be scheduled in a room of a community recreation building, house of worship, YMCA, YMHA, or storefront community action headquarters.

If you get parents together at your home, have someone take brief notes and get the name, address, and telephone number of those present. You will be able to get in touch with the same parents again and the notes will help you or someone else in the group to write a brief article on the meeting. The article may then be submitted to the school newsletter, your neighborhood or housing complex bulletin, the weekly shopper serving your area, or the local weekly newspaper. Include your name and phone number or those of another parent. Other parents of gifted children who read the article then know where to call if they would like to get together with you and your new-found friends.

Getting the Children Together

When the founder of the Gifted Child Society heard from other parents of gifted children in response to her ad in 1955, she not only invited the parents to meet each other, she also suggested that their children play together. One of the things that had made her "panicky" was the fact that her son didn't play with other children—youngsters of average abilities and interests in the neighborhood. In her conversations with respondents to the ad, she discovered other gifted children who also tended to be "loners."

This informal arrangement went on for about two years. The parents met occasionally and the children played together occasionally. The parents were pleased with what was happening with their children through the association with the other children. Not only did the youngsters play together, they read together, worked on projects together, and, perhaps most important, they stimulated each other with those endless questions. From time to time, the families joined forces to take the children on day trips to museums or historical sites.

The fathers of some of the children either worked for or knew someone who worked for an industry engaged in some form of research or manufacture. So, another addition to the still loose and unorganized "club" was a once-in-awhile Saturday field trip to a nearby plant or office building.

Taking the Big Step

None of the children in the "club" organized by the Society's founder was enrolled in an enrichment program at school. That was nearly unheard of back in the 1950s. About the only enrichment the children were getting was that provided by their informal play-work association with each other and the occasional trips planned by their parents. The parents decided it wasn't enough. To begin with, they were relying pretty much on their own gut reactions and their own wits. For all they knew, there were things they should be doing and weren't, or things they were doing but shouldn't.

If you are in the same boat as was this small band of parents in Bergen County, New Jersey, in the mid-fifties, you may have to make the same decision and take the same steps they did—organize your own formal enrichment program for gifted children. Much of this book will be devoted to answering the hows, whats, and whens about such a time-consuming and bewildering, but exciting, rewarding, and creative adventure.

Chapter 4

You Need to Organize

You have decided that you and other parents of gifted children in your school district or community need to organize and start your own enrichment program. That is probably the only simple decision you will make as long as the organization shall live. Those who have labored hard and long for the Gifted Child Society—many of them continuing to serve after their own children have "graduated" from the program—agree that no one has ever grown a callous while flying by the seat of his pants. Almost everyone has grown accustomed to the excitement—and loves it!

Setting Goals

Before the organizers do anything else, they should agree on some broad, overriding objectives. Building an organization and an educational program without objectives is like building a house without blueprints.

The objectives should fall into three categories: (1) those in behalf of gifted children served by the organization; (2) those in behalf of parents of gifted children served by the organization; and (3) those in behalf of *all* gifted children. The objectives listed below are offered for guidance only. Every organization should conceive its own objectives based on the deliberations of the organizers and on local needs.

1. To assist parents of gifted children served by the organization to better understand their children's special needs.

2. To advise parents of gifted children served by the organization how they can help enrich their children's lives at home.

21

3. To further enrich the lives of gifted children served by the organization by providing them with learning opportunities not available to them in the school they now attend.

4. To cooperate with and offer assistance to those public and private schools that provide or seek to provide appropriate education for gifted children.

5. To actively promote and encourage all public school systems and individual schools to provide appropriate education for gifted children.

6. To mount whatever informational program is necessary and feasible to educate the general public to the special needs of gifted children, the possible ways for fulfilling those needs, and the benefits accruing to society because of efforts made on behalf of gifted children.

7. To actively campaign among appropriate elected and appointed governmental and educational officials at the local, state, and federal levels to provide such laws, programs, and funding as are necessary to provide appropriate education for gifted children.

The objectives stated above sound simple, but it is no easy task for an organization to keep all of the objectives in mind all of the time and to strive for all of the objectives at the same time. Indeed, it is not always possible to obtain a consensus from members of the organization that every goal deserves attention. The minutes of meetings of the Gifted Child Society's executive board often contain reports of discussions about whether or how to accomplish certain objectives.

It requires the constant vigilance on the part of both officers and members of the organization to insure that actions and activities of the group always serve the objectives agreed on by all and not those of a few individuals. In the early days of the Society there were members who used the Society to further their own plans for a private school for gifted children, plans that had never been agreed to by the total membership as important to achieving its goals.

Think Big, But Start Small

Start small and make all your mistakes little ones. Your organization probably could make no greater mistake than to take on more than it can handle. Even in their consideration of broad objectives for the group, the officers and members might decide that it would be foolhardy to attempt at the start keeping all objectives in the air at the same time. It's likely that the novice jugglers will lose track of at least a couple of goals and the whole act might come to an untimely and inglorious end. Besides, it is highly doubtful, for example, that a brand-new organization of parents of gifted children trying to find its own direction can offer sound direction and wise counsel to public school educators or to state house representatives.

The high-priority objectives are those that serve the interests and needs of a reasonable number of gifted children and their parents. But even in meeting these objectives, the new organization should not attempt too much too soon. If the group grows too fast, the organization will lose control of the quality of its efforts. It is unrealistic to start out as novices with an extensive educational program and expect to maintain excellence. Among the problems, of course, are finding space for the educational program, qualified teachers to teach a variety of courses, and people who are willing and able to coordinate such an ambitious effort. Be too conservative rather than too enterprising. The Gifted Child Society had only a handful of children enrolled in its initial activities of the late fifties. And as late as 1963, the first summer workshop started with only thirty-six children.

If your organization chooses to profit from the experience of the Gifted Child Society, it will measure all its actions and decisions against its ability to cope with the consequences. The establishment of criteria for children eligible for the enrichment program provided by the group greatly affects how large the organization will be. Ditto for publicity. Don't live dangerously and endanger the life of the organization and its educational program by engaging in an all-out publicity and promotional campaign at the start. Extensive publicity about the organization and its educational program will cause an overwhelming response and ultimately be undermining.

The Gifted Child Society controls the enrollment in its workshop program to prevent its growing faster than its ability to handle growth. We would caution against sending promotional materials and news articles to large newspapers and educational journals at the start. Begin by reporting the activities of your organization to small dailies and weekly newspapers. It takes a lot of time to get something really good going. We decided that we would rather make our mistakes in private.

If you're starting small, what is small? The Gifted Child Society existed for about six years as an organization of no more than several dozen parents and their children. By the time the Society was ready to expand its educational program and overall activities, there were officers and members who had four or more years experience. They understood the problems of implementing an educational program and running a self-sufficient group without going into bankruptcy and without losing members who had given up in desperation or given out because of overwork.

When the group is small, those in charge have to be dedicated to making the organization work. If they aren't, the organization will die as quickly as it was born. Years later, when the organization has grown strong from withstanding many trials and surviving many mistakes, when experienced and/or paid personnel are in charge of day-to-day operations, members assume that they can afford to pay less attention and become less involved. To start off large, then, might deprive the organization of the kind of dedication and commitment that is so vital to sustain life in the early stages and to insure successful growth later on.

Who's Eligible to Join?

Chapter 10 describes in detail how to set criteria for children admitted to the organization's educational program. But something has to be said here as well, because now is the time to ask the question, "Who shall people this organization?" The criteria for admission of children determines to a large extent the number of adult members in the organization. The Society finally settled on an IQ of 120 as one of the criteria for acceptance into its educational program. It did not consider such a criterion ideal, but it is one yardstick about which there is some knowledge and agreement. It should be pointed out that the Society's criteria, a minimum IQ of 120 and emotional maturity reasonable for the student's age, have served it well. The 10,000 children and youth served by Society programs over the years have been those children the Society wanted to help and who were able to benefit from that help.

In recent years some members and officers of the Gifted Child Society have considered suggestions that it raise the IQ level now used as the cutoff point for children admitted to the program. By raising the IQ level, the number of children admitted would be reduced substantially. The suggestion that the IQ level be raised has been made from time to time by those who were concerned about the expansion of the organization and its program. One could not be blamed for assuming from this example that the new organization would do well to start off with very strict criteria that includes a higher IQ cutoff. But it ain't necessarily so.

The Gifted Child Society began with very inprecise criteria at a time when the population from which it might potentially draw members was in excess of half a million. Yet, the Society's growth was very slow. Why? Perhaps because it took so long to establish anything resembling a formal enrichment program. For three or four years, activities of the Society consisted mainly of occasional field trips and children coming together for play. Large numbers of people simply are not attracted to a small, loosely-knit organization offering an extremely limited program.

In a rural or sparsely settled area, a high IQ cutoff would so limit the group that it is doubtful whether there would be enough people to get the organization off the ground. Again, the group would do well to have less ambitious criteria that would insure enough people without inviting everyone.

To recap, determine who is eligible to join your organization . . .

• by the criteria established for the admission of children to the educational program.

• by the size and character of the educational program to be developed.

• by the publicity given to the activities of the organization.

• by the organizers' deciding whether they want to limit membership to a certain neighborhood, district, town, or region, and whether or not they want to attract as broad a representation as possible.

Should Professional Educators Be Members?

Back in the early 1960s, when the Society was still suffering from inexperience, a few angry and sarcastic parents drafted a questionnaire and sent it to all school superintendents in Bergen County. There are no copies of the questionnaire existing—extras have been buried in an unmarked grave. But we recall that it asked superintendents what they were doing for gifted children merely to prove the well-known point that they were not doing anything. Of the seventy questionnaires sent out, six were returned. Of the six replies, four were hostile and one was downright condemning. The sixth superintendent evidentally was not easily offended and he answered the questions to the best of his ability.

Among the lessons learned from the experience was that it is a futile and a potentially damaging exercise to ask questions for the sake of making a point instead of seeking information. Some members used the questionnaire to establish their belief that nothing much was being done for gifted children in the schools. If they had wanted to deliberately set the organization back, they could not have decided on a better plan. Another lesson learned from the experience was that a parent-run organization for gifted children needs professional educators more than professional educators need the organization.

The organization's dependence on professional educators is discussed at greater length in Chapter 6, but it should be stated here that professional educators should be welcome in the organization for the sake of the organization. Of course, we're talking about making members of educators who want to be contributing members to the organization. They can contribute much. We do not intend that educator members dominate the organization to the extent that laymen are no longer in a position to make decisions. Alas, in many PTAs the parent leaders have to clear all important business with the principal. He or she has an absolute veto. We're suggesting that parents and educators jointly conduct important business and that veto power be vested in an executive committee or, for some matters, in the total membership.

The Gifted Child Society found it much better to contact a few educators who could be identified as being sympathetic to special education for gifted children than to send membership applications out to every superintendent, principal, or teacher. Finding educators sympathetic to the cause should not be difficult. We suggest employing two means for selection: (1) watch local newspapers and state or regional educational journals for articles by or about educators in your area who show an interest in special education for gifted children; (2) ask parent members to suggest the names of teachers and administrators who they know to be concerned about appropriate education for gifted children.

Mrs. Marshall Lynn, an early organizer of the Society, was a high school math teacher who some of the parents knew as one who cared about gifted children and was herself gifted. A few years later, the parents leading the Society through its infancy, turned to Dr. Wm. Wendell Williams as a friend and adviser. Dr. Williams at the time was superintendent of a regional high school system. He had evidenced his concern for the gifted by starting an enrichment program in his school system and by writing and talking in public about the gifted child's needs and the ways those needs could be satisfied. It was no stroke of genius on the part of the parents when they asked Dr. Williams to be a consultant to the group, but it was a stroke of good fortune when, in a few years, Dr. Williams was asked to be president of the Society. It was during his four years as president that the Society grew up and broadened its educational program to reach many more children in the area.

Should educators be members? The organization can't afford to be without them. But make sure that they want to be there, that they have something to contribute, and that they can be contributing members wihout dominating the parent members.

Answering Parents' Gut Questions

At a recent seminar for parents of children enrolled in the Gifted Child Society's Saturday workshop, it was easy to distinguish the newcomers from the parents whose children had been enrolled for several years or had "graduated" from the Society's program. The new parents had many more questions than answers, and in the eyes of some you could still detect a look of panic or desperation. The new parent is very much like the mother who began organizing the Society back in the mid-fifties. You remember what she said: "One day I discovered my son was not of average intelligence and ability. I was panicky!" Because few people have any real training to be parents, parenthood can be a frightening and bewildering experience. If the typical parent has to ask someone at least 100 questions, the parent of a gifted child may have to get answers to at least 200.

From the beginning, the Gifted Child Society has considered it vital to satisfy the curiosity and relieve the anxiety of parents. The first school coordinator for the Society remembers back to the time when she took calls from parents. They primarily called her to sign up their children for courses, but many also used the occasion to ask questions. "My child is bored in school; what can I do to help him?" "I know my child is gifted, but he doesn't seem interested in doing anything; how can I get him moving?" "Our son keeps everybody else in the family on edge with his constant chatter and questioning; what can I do to prevent the rest of us from sitting on him?" "Our daughter is about to drop out of high school; what should we do?" And so it went. It seemed to the busy coordinator that she often spent more time answering questions or taking down questions for referral to others than she did signing up children for workshop courses. "It always seemed to me that parents really needed someone to talk to."

Indeed they do. And that's why for many years the Society has scheduled a series of parent seminars. Parents need basic information. They need to learn about their children and their own behavior toward their children. They need information about what the public schools are and are not doing for their children. They need to know what they can do on their own for their children, and what the organization's program can do for their children. As we've mentioned before, it helps a parent just to be able to sit down with other parents of gifted children and exchange problems, solutions, observations, and information gained through trial and error and through reading and asking the right questions of the right people.

We schedule parent discussion groups during the fall and spring workshops. While the children are busy in their courses, the parents gather to learn from experts and from each other. One of the first things your organization might do is establish parent discussion groups. It's important to do this even if the educational program for the children is minimal. If it's not convenient to schedule the seminars for times when the children are engaged in their activities, then schedule them at other times. But schedule them!

Here are some of the topics that have been the subject of Society discussion groups: the gifted child and his family; the kinds of behavior exhibited by gifted children; different methods for teaching gifted children; interpreting IQ tests; testing in general; trips to take and things to do with the gifted child; and what the federal, state, and local government are doing or planning for the gifted child and what parents can do to hurry things. Generally, discussion groups are led by people with expertise in the subject under discussion. Where do you find such people—and for free? The Society has never had a problem getting qualified leaders. Usually there are some members or their spouses who are qualified. That makes the job easy. If members are not qualified themselves, they often know of someone in the area who is. This is one of the times when educator members can be helpful. They can identify school or college educators and psychologists in the area who are knowledgeable and who will donate their services. Local representatives in the state government and officials of local or state education offices are often willing to speak if arrangements are made well in advance.

Other ways to answer parents' questions are by providing frequent opportunities for parents to question teachers, a lending library of books, pamphlets, and newspaper clippings on appropriate topics, and a question-and-answer section in the organization's newsletter.

The Society's library goes into business every Saturday morning when its workshops are in session for children. The librarian, one of the parents, sets up on tables and boxes in the hall outside the classrooms. Some books are donated, but most are purchased out of a small budget set aside for that purpose. There are now about 170 titles, and standard 3 by 5-inch cards are used to record who has taken what and when. Most of the books are picked for their value in helping parents understand their children. The librarian selects books for purchase by keeping track of new books published and listed daily in *The New York Times*, by scanning a variety of educational journals, and by jotting down titles suggested by Society members and teachers. The librarian also clips appropriate articles from newspapers and magazines and has them photocopied for lending. The ERIC Clearinghouse for Handicapped and Gifted supplies bibliographic abstracts of research papers and other materials. To contact the Clearinghouse, write:

> Council for Exceptional Children
> ERIC Clearinghouse for Handicapped and Gifted
> 1920 Association Drive
> Reston, Virginia   22091

Chapter 5

By-Laws and All That Jazz

Without by-laws there may be no guidelines for the organization to follow. Whenever the organization graduates from the status of an informal get-together serving a handful of parents and their children, it is time to look seriously at what would be best for the organization and the furtherance of its objectives. To help your organization take that serious look, it would be wise to seek the advice of a lawyer. The organization may be lucky enough to obtain the voluntary services of a member-lawyer or a lawyer-friend of a member. If you can't persuade a lawyer to donate his services, and you are forced to pay a fee, pay it. It will be worth it in the long run.

To Incorporate or Not

What are the advantages of incorporating your organization?

• Even the small organization will take in and spend money. If the organization is incorporated, any liabilities incurred will be those of the corporation and not of individuals in the organization.

• If the organization expects to employ teachers or other personnel, it is good protection for the personnel and the organization if it is the corporation employing people and not an informal group of people that can only be held accountable as individuals and not as a unit—a legal entity.

• Incorporation gives the organization legal status that enables it to deal more effectively with other corporations, institutions, and agencies. This is important if it is necessary to enter into a contract or formal agreement. It is less likely that the organization would be eligible for bank loans and governmental and foundation grants if it were not incorporated.

• By incorporating, the organization registers its official name, thereby preventing other groups from using the same or a similar name.

Laws governing corporations vary among the states. It is difficult, therefore, to be specific about many details that might affect the incorporation of your organization. Again the best advice the Society can give is to suggest getting someone else's advice—a lawyer's.

It is not necessary to issue stock in order to incorporate, and so there need be no stockholders. However, it generally is necessary and desirable to appoint and later elect a board of trustees for the corporation. When it incorporated, the Gifted Child Society named a number of distinguished educators throughout the nation as trustees—with their permission, of course. While the action lent prestige to the organization and its letterhead, it did not permit the trustees any real powers and responsibilities. And it was geographically impossible to ever call them into session. Your organization might consider asking six to ten prominent educators and laymen in your area to join the organization's officers as trustees. The trustees should meet annually for the purpose of appointing officers, and they should meet as often as necessary to review the organization's progress and offer direction for its future. The Society has amended its constitution and by-laws to provide for five trustees who represent the area served by the Society and who are able and willing to promote the aims of the Society.

Qualifying as a Non-Profit Organization

It is assumed that your organization will operate its educational program as a non-profit venture. In that case, the organization should apply to the Internal Revenue Service for official non-profit status, which will exempt the organization from paying any federal income or corporate taxes. Contact the IRS office in your area for help and necessary forms. Laws differ among the states, but in most cases the organization's non-profit status also will exempt it from paying state and local income, corporate and property taxes. Ask your lawyer for advice on state laws and local ordinances affecting the tax status of non-profit organizations.

Because the organization qualifies as a non-profit organization, members can deduct dues paid when filing their income tax returns. They cannot deduct tuition paid for instruction, however.

Drafting a Constitution and By-Laws

A football game without rules is not a football game, and an organization without a constitution and by-laws is not an organization.

The Gifted Child Society has been living with the same constitution and by-laws since 1964. Amendments are always possible as the organization grows. The constitution and by-laws were adopted in 1964 after careful scrutiny by a committee of members chaired by a member-lawyer. We stress most emphatically that it is vital to have a lawyer present for the deliberations when the organization is considering any important action that commits or binds the organization, its officers or members, or grants powers and responsibilities to officers and members.

The Society's amended constitution and by-laws are given in Appendix A, but it might be helpful to make a few observations about them in order to guide your organization in this important undertaking.

• The purpose of the organization as defined in the constitution and by-laws should be in accordance with the broad objectives adopted in the beginning by the membership.

• The Society chose to specify that the president of the organization be an educator, preferably, or a prominent public figure. The role of the professional educator will be discussed in Chapter 6, but the Society believes that a very capable and dedicated educator can be of immeasurable value to the organization as its leader. Another reason for specifying the criteria for president is the Society's belief that the president must not only be a leader of the organization but also must be capable of exercising leadership and commanding respect in the larger community. Your organization will have to measure the decision of the Society in this matter against your own experience and situation and your organizational goals.

• Responsibility for the operations of the organization should, for the most part, be delegated to an executive committee composed of officers and committee chairpersons. No organization invests the total membership with most of the responsibility for conducting the organization's business. If most businesss items must be submitted to the general membership for approval, the organization is liable to spend most of its time running in place.

• Important consideration should be given to the selection of standing committees. The chairpersons of these committees carry on a major share of the business of the organization.

• It is important to spell out how the annual budget will be drafted and approved. A significant provision of the Society's by-laws gives the executive board authority to operate the organization on an austerity budget if the membership fails to approve, or delays approval of, the proposed annual budget. Without such a provision, the organization could founder if a quorum cannot be mustered at several membership meetings or if a small group of opposition members works its will to stall passage of the budget.

• The Society's by-laws require chairpersons of standing committees to present an overall plan of action to the executive board before embarking on any activities. Such a provision allows elected and appointed officials to make sure committee work stays within the bounds of the organization's objectives. Neither time nor money are wasted on activities that have no chance for sanction by the board or the general membership.

The organization's constitution and by-laws may serve for a long time, but remember, they are not written on stone tablets. Important points may have been overlooked at the first drafting, conditions change, goals are re-evaluated, and so on. It is important, therefore, that the constitution and by-laws be subjected to periodic review—at least every three or four years. If after the review, the appropriate committee recommends no amendments, so be it.

Just as the constitution and by-laws are not to be considered as being everlasting, they also should not be considered as restraints. Make them a design for good administration and effective operations, not rules aimed at preventing bad administration and ineffective operations. The emphasis should be on encouraging what's good and right, rather than on discouraging what might be bad and wrong. The constitution and by-laws must allow the organization to grow and change.

Chapter 6

Workers Needed

Recently, a New Jersey high school PTA sent a letter to parents. The letter explained that the organization was getting nowhere for lack of leadership. If someone would only volunteer to be officers, said the letter, the organization could get moving. It's still too early to tell whether the plea succeded, but it's doubtful. Blanket appeals rarely work. In this chapter, we hope to advise your organization how to go about setting up its leadership structure and how to get people to volunteer their talents and time—lots of it.

What Officers Are Needed?

There are organizations in which the officers outnumber the members. There are groups that elect half a dozen or more vice presidents and give each a committee to head. Then there are organizations that give certain people titles simply to have them around at executive board meetings so their fertile brains can be picked clean.

If your organization starts small, and we assume it will, it probably will not want to begin with the number of officials who now govern and administer the Gifted Child Society. So, we'll start off by describing the necessary officials for any organization, and then we'll talk about a structure for the future. In all of this, we're assuming that the main purpose of the organization is to create and operate an out-of-school enrichment program for children of members. Along the way, however, we will refer to additional activities officers might turn their attention to while still keeping within the overall objectives of the organization.

If an organization consisted of only a man and his wife who wanted to offer their only child an individualized enrichment program, the chances are one of them would become president of the

34

organization and the other secretary-treasurer. These days don't bet that the man would be president. Women don't—and shouldn't—automatically become secretaries. The three offices mentioned are the crucial ones. The president is needed to guide the organization, to be responsible for making sure other officers and committee chairpersons do their job. In other words, the president makes sure the organization swims instead of sinks. The secretary and treasurer are necessary if the organization is going to know what it has done, what it's supposed to do, whether it was able to afford what has already been done, and whether it can afford what remains to be done. We will describe these jobs in a little more detail shortly.

When the Society was in its infancy and offering courses to a small number of children, a number of parents were involved in the organization of the educational program and in the registration of children. Indeed, there was a different registrar for each course. Parents who wanted to enroll their child in science called one person, and parents who wanted to enroll their child in creative writing called somebody else. It wasn't easy on parents enrolling their children in several courses, and it wasn't easy on the organization trying to keep track of what everybody was doing.

It is suggested, therefore, that the position of school coordinator be created at the start, even if your organization conducts only two or three courses for thirty or so children. One person has to be responsible for this most vital function, and the best time to break someone in is while the organization and the educational program are still small. If he or she can learn the ropes when there isn't all that much to do, hopefully, that person will be prepared for the time when there will seem to be too much to do. This should be a part-time salaried position, the salary being based on and paid from tuition.

The new organization, then, needs a president, a secretary, a treasurer, and a school coordinator. The jobs of secretary and treasurer could be combined at the start, but separate them before the load becomes too cumbersome. Don't forget, we're talking about people volunteering for positions as officers. Parents will work hard if they think it benefits their children, but don't press them too hard or don't take unfair advantage of them. It's a much wiser and safer course to add new positions rather than to continually pile work upon the shoulders of a few dedicated, but sagging, bodies. If the shoulders of the overworked few drop too low, the organization could slide off and shatter like Humpty Dumpty.

People can become tired and bored with their jobs. Or they can grow stale in them. In either case, it's healthy for the organization and for the officers too, if new blood is pumped in to replace tired blood. The leaders need to be fresh, enthusiastic, and sharp. The presidents and committees in future years would do well to recall this advice and make their decisions accordingly.

As the organization grows, it will be necessary to add more officers. One of the first additions should be a vice president. It can be argued that a vice president should be named from the start. We don't disagree. In naming the crucial officers, we did not include back-up personnel. Your organization may want to have a second team from the very beginning. If so, fine. You may want to have not only a vice president but also an assistant secretary and assistant treasurer.

The vice president is essentially a back-up person. He is available to stand in if the president should be unable to perform any of his functions. Nationally, there has been much discussion in recent years about the way in which we choose a vice president for the federal government. It has been argued that the vice president should have all of the qualifications of the President since he or she is only a "heartbeat away" from being President. There's no need to be quite so dramatic about the position of vice president for your organization, but we do suggest that candidates for vice president have the same qualities you look for in your president. Even if the vice president is only called upon to conduct the meetings of the executive committee or board from time to time, it can be detrimental to the organization if he has neither the inclination nor the ability to take charge and run a productive meeting. We will talk more about vice presidents when we discuss the duties and responsibilities of officers in more detail.

As the organization expands, it probably will be necessary not only to make the secretary and treasurer separate jobs but also to create two secretarial positions. Many organizations have both a recording secretary and a corresponding secretary. We suggests the two positions only when it becomes plain that one secretary has too much to do. We don't advocate the creation of jobs for the sake of giving people titles or because other groups have them.

When the organization reaches the point that it is offering many courses and employing many teachers, it is time to consider the position of curriculum coordinator. What the educational program will need as it grows is a first-rate administrator who is an educator. The curriculum coordinator should be a part-time salaried person appointed by the executive body or board of trustees.

The last addition to your organization's roster of officers and administrators will be an executive director. The executive director is the last position, not the least. The position is the last one to be created because it is not until the organization grows very large that it becomes necessary to have an executive director. The Gifted Child Society did not establish the position of executive secretary, now director, until the fall of 1970—more than a dozen years after the organization's modest beginning. By that time the Society had enrolled almost 500 children in its Saturday workshops. It was also then that the organization began making a concerted effort toward achieving one of its goals—to work in behalf of all gifted children among the public, educators, and legislators. There was simply too much business—phone calls, correspondence, reports, speaking requests, etc.—for elected officers engaged in full-time work elsewhere to handle.

Your organization may not want to wait until the educational program is serving 500 children before appointing and paying a part-time or full-time executive director. But, in making the decision, keep one eye on the budget and one eye on the workload of elected officers and volunteer workers. As in the case of the school coordinator and the curriculum coordinator, the executive director's salary can be wholly or partially paid out of tuition income. But the organization will be able to get just so much out of tuition income without making course fees so high that they keep out some gifted children, which would be self-defeating.

When our school coordinator was first appointed, the position paid a dollar-fifty per course unit. If a child was enrolled in two courses, the school coordinator would be paid three dollars. The position now pays two twenty-five per course unit. The curriculum coordinator's position was established in the spring of 1970, and the salary was originally five-hundred dollars per semester. That salary has now increased to $1,650 a year. When the executive secretary's position was created, it paid $1,500 a year.

What Should Officers' Duties Be?

Officers' duties are spelled out briefly in the Society's constitution and by-laws (Appendix A). The official job description of the three salaried, part-time Society administrators— executive director, school coordinator, and curriculum coordinator—are given in Appendix C. But anyone who has read a job description and has then gone out to do the job knows that the official outline refers only to some of the principal responsibilities and duties. A candidate running for president of the United States who thought the job was pretty well spelled out by the Constitution would be in for a rude shock the day after the inauguration. Also, the job descriptions say nothing about the kind of person needed for the position—his abilities, attitudes, and resources. The people of the nation would be hard pressed to decide between candidates for president if they measured them only against the qualifications listed in the Constitution.

In this section we'll tell you what many of the jobs are *really* like and what kinds of qualities it takes to perform the duties best. We'll begin with the officers.

President

The constitution and by-laws of the Gifted Child Society say, as do most organizations' constitution and by-laws, that the president shall "preside" over general membership meetings and meetings of the executive board. The dictionary gives two definitions of "preside." First, to "occupy" a place of leadership, and second, to "exercise guidance, direction, or control." Perhaps the most important quality a president can have is to recognize the difference between the two definitions and emphasize the second one. The person who sits in the president's chair and allows the business of the organization to pass before him in disorder is like the movie director who sits in his chair and allows the action to happen at the whim of actors and cameramen.

A good president is one who exercises control over the meetings of members and officers to the extent necessary to make them as productive as possible. This does not mean the president should be a dictator, or that members and other officers should be seen but not heard. Suppose the curriculum coordinator and the chairman of the curriculum committee report that they have been unable to meet and decide on courses for the upcoming semester, and the deadline for publicizing the program is drawing near. The president must step in to make sure that a meeting of the curriculum committee is scheduled on the spot and that the curriculum coordinator calls him immediately after the meeting to report the results. If and when the organization has an executive director, the president may delegate this follow-up role.

The good president does not allow discussions or proposals from members, officers or administrators to drag the organization away from that business aimed at fulfilling the principal objectives. Indeed, the Society's constitution and by-laws say that the president should perform whatever duties are necessary "in order that the objects and purposes of this Society may be fulfilled."

Perhaps the most important contribution any president can make is to bring order and compromise out of confusion and conflict. People can get hung up on their own theories and ideas. They get to arguing among themselves and get nowhere. Somebody has to bring everyone together and have them come up with a compromise plan that will satisfy all, or nearly all.

This kind of strong leadership must be exercised expertly and carefully, however. The key is to keep everyone involved, building on their strengths and guiding them toward solutions.

Vice President

We've already described the vice president as a back-up to the president and we've mentioned the necessity for choosing someone with similar qualities of leadership. But in an organization without an executive director and/or such other administrators as curriculum coordinator and school coordinator, the vice president can assist the president in exercising strong leadership. The president might suggest to the vice president that he work closely with three or four committees to keep them active and working toward the right objectives.

The president may delegate to the vice president responsibility for developing contacts with educators, political leaders, and others who can assist in the fulfillment of the organization's objectives. On the other hand, if the president is the kind of person who can function best while publicly promoting the interests of all gifted children, the vice president may be given more responsibility for the internal operations of the organization and its educational program.

The Society's constitution and by-laws provide for two vice presidents. In the early days of the organization both officers assumed specific administrative duties along with the president. After the Society created the salaried positions of school coordinator, curriculum coordinator, and, finally, executive director, the vice presidents were called on less to perform as administrators.

Secretaries

Every organization needs at least one very good secretary. The Society's constitution and by-laws say that the recording secretary shall "record the minutes of all regular and executive board meetings." But, if you've been in several different organizations, you know there are minutes and then there are minutes. Some secretaries miss half the important resolutions introduced and passed; some don't miss any resolutions but also don't miss recording every immaterial discussion and every inconsequential statement. In between the extremes is the secretary who knows what is important and knows how important it is to get such business recorded fully and accurately. And she or he knows what to exclude.

Some years ago the executive board devoted an entire meeting to a debate about the pros and cons of having a private school for gifted children. The recording secretary listened to the hours of spirited discussions and eventually noted in the minutes of the meeting that "a discussion on a private school for the gifted proved inconclusive."

It is especially vital to record in the official minutes those actions that decide policy and direction, authorize the collection or expenditure of money, and prescribe what duties people will perform. And it is important that there is sufficient information recorded so that people looking back at the minutes are able to determine why certain actions were taken. For example, it isn't enough to report that Archibald Fairchild was appointed executive director on July 4, 1976 at a salary of $1,500. The minutes should record that Mr. Fairchild was among fifteen candidates for the job who were screened by a committee of officers and members headed by the president; that his term is for one year; that his duties have been defined; and that a copy of the job description is attached. It might also be desirable to attach to the minutes a brief ·résumé for Mr. Fairchild.

Without a good set of minutes, succeeding officers will be severely handicapped as they try to build for the future on what has been done in the past. They may be placed in very embarrassing positions if disputes over past actions should arise, as they certainly will from time to time.

Treasurer

A discussion of the treasurer's duties is given in Chapter 8.

School Coordinator

A discussion of the school coordinator's role is given in Chapter 13.

Curriculum Coordinator

The duties of curriculum coordinator are given in Chapters 11 and 12.

Executive Director

The executive director is the chief administrator and assumes many of the duties of the president in a large organization. One of the prime duties the executive director assumes from the president and vice presidents is that of overseeing the work of committees, other administrators, and other officers. The job description drafted for the Society's executive director says that the person holding the position "is responsible for the business of the Society being conducted according to its constitution." As already noted, this is a responsibility usually given to the president.

The Society also saw fit to point out that the executive director "in the absence of the president represents the Society to outside agencies and the public at large." In the last few years the Society's executive director has made many contacts throughout New Jersey and the nation and has attended many meetings and workshops as the Society extends its influence and offers its experience in the effort to serve all gifted children.

What should you look for in an executive director? For one thing, you should look for someone who doesn't mind turning his or her house into an office. Because where the executive director is, so is the office, unless the organization is large and affluent enough to rent an office. If the executive director's family doesn't mind the organization's business being conducted from their home, the very least that should be done by the organization is to install a separate phone for the organization.

We're not being facetious when suggesting that the executive director's capacity to function out of the home is important. It will do no good to hire a crackerjack person who simply can't function out of a make-do office and is weighed down and worn out by either excessive family responsibilities or family pressure.

Our executive director came into the Society as a parent of children in the educational program. That was about ten years ago. She has had many positions in the organization since joining. What makes her especially valuable to the Society in her present job is experience and familiarity with the way the organization operates—and a lot of dedication. But the current school coordinator and curriculum coordinator came to their jobs from outside the organization and are serving with distinction. Whether your organization chooses to turn first to its parents or whether it goes outside the membership to fill a salaried position is a decision that has to be weighed carefully. Regardless of your decision, however, here are points to consider when selecting an executive director:

1. The person must be sincerely dedicated to the cause of providing educational enrichment for gifted children. Anyone who seeks the post strictly for the income will not only be disappointed but won't fulfill the expectations nor satisfy the needs of the organization.

2. The person must be able to get parents to volunteer their time and to work hard, and to get other administrators and teachers to work hard for very little money. This means the executive director must be able to pleasantly and gently, but firmly, move along the business of the organization. The executive director must be skilled at compromise and at making others look and feel good.

3. The person must be capable of properly representing the organization in contacts with groups, educators, political leaders, and others outside the organization. This means that the executive director must be able to prepare and deliver a position paper, express the ideas and proposals of the organization accurately and convincingly, and answer questions quickly and fully. He or she must like people!

As an example of the kind of duties the executive director might perform that would require the abilities mentioned above, here are some of the recent activities of our executive director: (1) she testified before a U.S. Senate sub-committee; (2) she appeared as an expert at a workshop sponsored by the New Jersey State Department of Education; (3) she escorted visiting educators through the Society's Saturday workshop; (4) she worked closely with a large group of school superintendents to prepare a questionnaire designed to elicit information about what schools are doing for gifted children; and (5) she served as a participant at a seminar in California sponsored by the U.S. Office of Education.

When your organization is ready for an executive director, it is ready to pay someone a minimal salary to do a monumental job. The organization must be ready to take its place among those agencies and individuals throughout the country who are making waves on behalf of gifted children.

Picking the Right Committees and Chairpersons

The standing committees of the Gifted Child Society are listed in the constitution and by-laws (Appendix A). Chairpersons are appointed by the president. For the beginning organization, the critical committees probably are curriculum, finance, publicity, and workshop activities.

It might be useful to look at these committees a little more closely.

Curriculum

We'll be talking in later chapters about the educational program, but it should be pointed out here how vital the curriculum committee is to the early success of the program. The curriculum committee, particularly before the appointment of a curriculum coordinator, has the prime responsibility for these major activities: designing a format for the educational program, suggesting courses, interviewing prospective teachers, suggesting teachers to hire, and evaluating courses and the performance of teachers.

Because of the duties assumed by the committee, it is desirable to have as members parent-educators.

Finance

Members of the finance committee are responsible for maintaining a close watch on where money is coming from and where it is going. It could be called a watchdog committee, but it should also be a planning committee.

In cooperation with the treasurer and with other officers, the committee should review past financial policies and spending practices to determine how well the organization has accomplished its goals with the funds available. Then it should plan for the future to determine what income will be needed to support expansion of the organization and extension of its work toward its objectives. Such planning is invaluable to the organization. If the executive board is considering hiring a school coordinator and/or curriculum coordinator, the finance committee could study what tuition will be needed to accommodate the expenditures and whether the increased tuition will still attract the membership the organization intends to serve.

Publicity

Chapter 14 deals with publicity, but it should be pointed out to the new organization that the publicity committee is important to establish at the start. The committee should be in charge not only of how the organization communicates to the public but also any advertising or promotion undertaken by the organization.

The committee should be asked to develop communications policy as well as execute it, and it should also consider how much or how little the organization wants to publicize itself and its educational program. The Gifted Child Society might have grown faster than it wanted to had it decided early to gain as much public notice as possible through the news media, advertising, and other forms of promotion. The committee, then, should come up with a communications policy based on the goals the organization's leaders and members have set.

To staff this committee look among the membership for newspaper reporters and editors, television and radio newspeople, those who have worked as publicity chairmen for other organizations, advertising account executives, photographers, commercial artists, printers, graphics experts, and copy editors.

Workshop Activities Committee

This committee can be a very critical one at the start. If the organization decides it does not want to pay a school coordinator from the beginning to be in charge of enrolling students in courses, then this committee can take charge of course registration. As we have mentioned, when the Society began, there were individual registrars for each course offered. We don't recommend this as a way to operate, but it is better than having no system at all.

If a school coordinator has been hired, the members of the workshop committee still assist by helping the coordinator in operating the educational program and by working with him or her to establish new policy and procedures. Suppose the registration forms being used are not doing the job the school coordinator expected they would do. The workshop committee might undertake a study of the registration procedure and the problems connected with the existing forms. Then they would be in a position to recommend new approaches and new forms to the executive board.

The workshop committee needs no specialized personnel, although it is always helpful if some members have been in charge of registration for some other organization. Experience is never to be overlooked.

Whom do you look for as committee chairpersons? The people the organization selects as committee chairpersons should have these things in their favor:

• *Experience.* It is helpful if at least the chairperson of any committee has had previous experience and/or training in doing what he's going to do for your organization.

• *Time.* The chairpersons of most committees wind up doing most of the work. He or she, therefore, should be able and willing to give up time for meetings, phone calls, and report writing. There will be meetings of both the committee and the executive board to attend.

• *Creativity.* The chairperson should be able to come up with ideas to help the committee and the organization perform more effectively.

• *Leadership ability.* The chairperson can cut down on his or her own time if the committee members can be made to contribute their fair share of time and energy. The chairperson with leadership ability knows how to delegate work and how to monitor the performance of others.

Tapping the Talent of Parents

No matter what has needed doing, we've had people to do it—without exception. And there have always been six more behind them. Very few people have turned down requests to help. If they do turn us down, it's probably because they *really* are too busy.

To simplify the job of finding and using talent among organization members, the Society has parents fill out an information form about themselves when they register their children for the program. Parents list their interests, relevant experience, and full-time work, and are requested to state what Society committees they would be willing to serve on.

Here is an example of how we use the information cards filled out by parents. While reviewing the cards on one occasion, we noticed that a mother of a child enrolled in the Saturday enrichment program had expressed a very strong desire to become involved with the curriculum of the Saturday workshop. The woman was called on the telephone and invited to the next meeting of the executive board. After the meeting, she showed so much enthusiasm for and interest in curriculum planning that we named her to the curriculum committee. She later turned out to be one of the best committee chairpersons in the history of the Society.

But even with all there is to do, the organization does not tap its parent talent to its fullest. Out of about one-thousand families, only fifty or so are actively working on committees or in some other capacity. Of course, more families may be used for a one-time phone campaign.

However, when the Society was just beginning, when there was no executive director, no school coordinator, and no curriculum coordinator, everybody worked. They had to. They wanted to. They worked for their own children and for the organization. When the group is small, members tend to work harder for the organization because it is necessary for its very survival. As the organization grows and prospers and salaried administrators are appointed, members feel less concern for the welfare of the organization. They expect it to take pretty good care of itself without their help.

Don't expect all volunteer workers to attend meetings. Some are more than willing to pitch in and put in long hours, but they have an aversion to meetings or crowds or to just going out of the house. Use them anyway. Most people have never seen the woman who does most of the typing for our organization. She prefers not to mingle. So, she isn't pressed to mingle. The Society is simply thankful for her work.

Once a month, or according to some other schedule, your organization's executive board—officers, administrators, and committee chairpersons—should meet to conduct the business of the organization. Here are some tips that might help the meetings be more productive and run more smoothly:

Tip 1

Give everyone a chance to speak who wants to speak. Don't allow one person or a few people to dominate.

Tip 2

Give credit to people when credit is due them. A simple thank you for a job performed or for a contribution made in time, energy and ideas can go far to make people feel happy and feel like performing and contributing again. Where appropriate and possible, thanks should be expressed publicly at a membership meeting, in a newsletter, or in a news release.

Tip 3

Make up an agenda in advance of each board meeting and send it to all members of the board. By having an agenda, officers, administrators, and committee chairpersons know what is expected of them and what is considered important.

Tip 4

Stick to the agenda insofar as possible. By following the agenda, you give credence to advance planning, and you allow people to know at any given time during the meeting what has been accomplished and what is left to do. The agenda should call for specific times to begin and adjourn. These times should be adhered to as strictly as possible. To be fair to everyone, those who are present on time should not have to wait fifteen minutes or half an hour for the tardy ones to arrive. Nor is it fair to people who have to drive far, relieve a baby sitter, or arise at six A.M. to keep them an hour or two past the agreed closing time.

Tip 5

The president or executive director can do wonders for morale on the board if he or she will, (1) the day after the meeting, telephone those involved in controversy and heated debate to make sure there are no lasting hurts; (2) telephone those who did not make a meeting for unexplained reasons to see if they are sick or feel uncomfortable attending meetings; and (3) telephone brand-new board members to find out if they are comfortable in their roles at the meeting. Try to be very patient and helpful, because things will run more smoothly in the long run.

We think the organization needs as its leader a professional educator who knows about programs for the gifted and has had experience with gifted children as a school administrator. The laymen

of the Society were so grateful for the leadership of the organization's first educator-president that they made it a requirement in the
constitution and by-laws that the president, if at all possible, be an
educator. The parents who helped shape the Society through the years
agree to a man and a woman that it was professional know-how that
got the organization where it is today. Many parents' groups that
have started without the support and guidance of any educators have
failed.

How does the professional educator help?

• If the educator has both a commitment to helping gifted children and experience in designing programs for them, he or she can
show the parents the way. He or she can also suggest alternative
ways to go and parents can decide the direction.

• The educator provides the necessary link between the private
organization and the schools. Some parents in the Society remember
the days when there were those leaders of the group who carried a
very big chip on their shoulder and estranged the public schools and
public school educators. The reasoning seemed to be that if the public
schools couldn't or wouldn't do more for their children, then to hell
with them.

Earlier we talked about a questionnaire that was sent to educators in Bergen County, New Jersey. That questionnaire convinced
some administrators that they were right all along not to trust a
group of pushy parents and their smart kids. To show how far the
group has come in its relations with educators, a recent questionnaire
to public schools went out with the blessing of the county organization of school superintendents and with their coporation in its
preparation (see Appendix D).

In the early days of the Society most parents came to the organization as the result of reading about the educational program in
the newspapers. Today most parents are referred to the Society by
their child's teacher or principal. Cooperation with the public schools
has paid off for the organization, but more importantly it has paid
off for the children the Society is dedicated to serve.

• Educators in the organization are better able to suggest worthwhile courses for the children. And they know where to find qualified
teachers for the educational program. This is an exceptional plus,
especially in view of the fact that there are still states that do not

have teachers trained specifically for teaching gifted children. Naturally, parents also can identify good teachers for the program, but educators are still the best source.

• The Society's first educator-president not only provided strong leadership when it was needed, he provided a place to meet—in one of the schools he administered. And his secretary was the Society's "executive secretary" and all-around Gal Friday for a long time. Even if the educator in the group cannot supply a meeting place, he is a good link to other educators who can supply space for the educational program and membership meetings.

• The educator in a position of leadership gives the organization and its educational program status among educators in the area being served. It gives your group the kind of legitimacy it desperately needs to succeed.

Your organization may choose not to have an educator as president, or as any officer for that matter, but you certainly should have educators as active trustees and members. Your organization should look to them frequently for advice and leadership in the areas suggested.

The life you save may be that of your organization.

Chapter 7

If Money Doesn't Grow on Trees,
Where Does It Come From?

Whatever the obstacles to starting an organization similar to ours, lack of money is not one of them. Money has never been a problem for the Gifted Child Society in its long history. That's not because it was founded by wealthy individuals who contributed from their own great assets. On the contrary, the Society was founded by parents who contributed great amounts of time and energy, but paid only their dues. Perhaps some paid for more business calls than they should have, or forgot to bill the organization for typing paper or index cards, but no one has ever had to dip into or hers own savings or write out a personal check to keep the organization solvent.

Do You Need Investment Capital?

The Gifted Child Society has never had and has never sought investment capital. It has never had and has never asked for a bank loan. The only grant it ever sought or received from any governmental agency or foundation was the one that allowed it to prepare this book. Investment capital was not needed because costs have always been minimal and always in keeping with the income. Here is why:

1. The Society has never rented office space and has never rented or bought such office equipment as desks, chairs, or electric typewriters.

2. The Society didn't pay any administrator for running the organization until more than twelve years after the group started. Even then, the executive director's salary was more a token of appreciation than a realistic wage.

3. Administrators' and teachers' salaries have been paid directly by tuition received from parents enrolling their children in the educational program.

4. The educational program has always been conducted in rented space in a public school or church building. In the case of the public schools, the rent has been low. The church donated its space. The church facilities were used in the early days of the Society, when only a few rooms were needed.

Assessing Dues

In the beginning, the Society enrolled children in the educational program, small as it was, without requiring their parents to join the Society and pay dues. That policy changed in the early 1960s, and we recommend that your organization charge dues from the start. Parents in the early 1960s were required to join as members of the Society and pay family dues of three dollars per year. The three dollars covered only the costs of postage, telephone, stationery, and printing of class schedules. By 1964, the dues were up to five dollars. They also paid for increased publicity and advertising and the fees of outstanding speakers at membership meetings. Today, the dues are eight dollars per year per family. The Society believes they are still a bargain in view of what eight dollars buys in today's inflation.

For its dues the member family receives two newsletters each year, brochures announcing courses for the fall and spring workshops and the summer session, parent seminars, membership meetings, and free use of the lending library. Most important, of course, the dues help pay the costs of running the organization.

How to Afford and Grant Scholarships

The Society's scholarship program started late and slow. It started late because in the early years officers and members were busy just breathing life into the organization. It started slow because public school officials did not respond. In order to attract candidates for scholarships the minimum IQ standard of 120 was waived and a scholarship candidate was admitted on the basis of teacher recommendation only. The Society sent a letter to more than 200 principals in the area served by the Society, explaining the educational program, the scholarship plan, the waiving of the IQ criterion, and even offered to arrange door-to-door transportation for any scholarship child. It was suggested to the schools that they select bright children from among those youngsters who qualified for special assistance under Title I of the Elementary and Secondary Education Act, designed for low-income and minority children. Special follow-up calls were made to principals in communities where there was the greatest number of eligible children. In spite of these efforts, it has taken the scholarship program nearly five years to gain attntion in the public schools.

The first scholarship student was one who was financed by a teachers' association in a local school district. All other scholarship students have been funded out of the Society treasury. This past year the Society financed twenty-five children. The schools are now doing better in identifying and recommending candidates.

Until recently, scholarships were financed strictly out of tuition. But we decided it wasn't right for parents of some children to pay extra to finance scholarships for other children. The Society now plans a series of fund-raising activities for the scholarship program. One such activity, for example, sold pictures of the summer session to parents of children enrolled. The photographs were taken by a professional photographer who is a member. Naturally, he donated his services. The Society also is talking to some businesses about the possibility of their sponsoring scholarship students.

The scholarship program has never been advertised, although it has been reported in news articles about the work of the Society. It has not been advertised because of the requirement that a school verify the economic status of the applicant and the child's intellectual and emotional qualifications.

See figures 2 and 3 for the letter to public school administrators about the scholarship program and the form used by the school to recommend a scholarship candidate.

Even though in the past the Society was never able to set aside special funds for scholarships, the organization has never denied a scholarship to any child applying for the Saturday workshops.

FIGURE 2

THE SATURDAY WORKSHOPS

Sponsored by the Gifted Child Society, Inc.

(A Non-Profit Organization)

Dear School Administrator:

Thank you for your interest in our scholarship program. The information below will help you and your staff select those students for whom the program was developed.

Economic Criteria:

Criteria for economic need should be similar to the criteria used in the selection of students for participation in the Title I (ESEA) Program and/or determined by the administration, school social worker or school nurse.

Intellectual Criteria:

Our goal is to involve students with high intellectual potential in order to supplement their present school experiences.

The usual intellectual criterion for participation in our Workshops is an I.Q. of 120 or more. However, this criterion may not be applicable to those students we hope to reach in our scholarship program. Therefore, when necessary, the recommendation of scholarship students will be dependent upon your and/or your staff's judgment of a candidate's intellectual potential, and the recommendations from you and/or your particular staff may be submitted.

Registration:

Please use the enclosed enrollment forms. The number of students who will receive scholarships is limited, and applications will be processed in the order in which they are received. Registration closes one week before the first Saturday of the semester. However, many of our Workshop classes reach capacity earlier.

Please address all your questions to our school coordinator.

Thank you for being involved with our scholarship program.

encl: Enrollment Forms

FIGURE 3

THE SATURDAY WORKSHOPS

Sponsored by the Gifted Child Society

ENROLLMENT FORM

Scholarship Program

....

Family Name...................................Husband...................Wife...................

Child's First Name...

Birthday.. Grade.......................... Age...............

Address.. Phone..........................
         Street   Town   Zip

Father's Occupation........................ Mother's Occupation..........................

Child's School................................. Principal..................................

School Address.. Phone...............................

Special Interest of Child ....
                        (To be used for Workshop course selection)

Reasons for recommending this child and additional comments:

....

....

....

....

....
                          (Signature)

This enrollment form must be completed and mailed to our School Coordinator.

Registration closes.. Class sizes are limited, so please enroll early to avoid disappointments.

Registration acknowledgement postal cards giving course time and room number will be sent to parents after registration closing.

Chapter 8

Keeping Track of the Money

About $89,000 passed in and out of the Gifted Child Society treasury in one year recently. It's a significant increase over the cash flow of the late 1950s. In those days we had no ledgers or audits. In fact the treasurer in 1963 inherited a check book, period. There were no receipts, no cancelled bills, no financial records of any kind, and no books in which to enter income and expenses.

An accountant would have had nightmares if he thought about the amount of money we turned over in small checks without direction or order, but somehow it has all worked out. The fact that it has does not mean that a new organization starting out should maintain no records or books. On the contrary, we emphatically recommend that the organization have a ledger at the beginning and keep good financial records.

Who does the organization look for as treasurer? Our first treasurer was a bookkeeper for a bank and had maintained books for other organizations, but she asked her brother, the treasurer of a corporation, to set up the books for her. The current treasurer is a bank executive. The treasurer definitely should have had some experience either in business or in other organizations that maintain financial books and draft budgets.

What does the treasurer do? The Society's present treasurer makes entries in the ledger and prepares all checks for the Society. Once a month he prepares a simple treasurer's report (see fig. 4) and submits it to the executive board. Once a year he prepares a

55

financial statement for the Internal Revenue Service, even though the Society as a non-profit organization pays no income or corporate taxes. The annual statement must be audited. The treasurer's time is spent in this way: His duties require about half a day once a week for eight months of the year and about an hour during the other four months. The extra time is spent approximately two months before and after the fall and spring workshops and the summer session.

Setting up the Books

Your organization's treasurer, or financial adviser, probably will have his or her own ideas about setting up the books. Your ledger columns might be different in some respects from the Society's, but the procedures the Society follows might be of help.

There are two sections of the ledger. The sections might be headed debits and credits, or income and expenses, or, in the case of the Society's books, income and disbursements.

These are the categories under income:

1. Income from tuition and dues. Because this income is in the form of small checks, a number of checks are combined for one entry total. For example, suppose $4,000 worth of tuition and dues checks are to be recorded as income at the same time. Rather than spend the time and use the space to record each check individually, the checks are recorded on an adding machine tape and only the total is entered in the ledger. The machine tape is kept as a record. Part of the treasurer's records are statements from the school coordinator that indicate which families have paid dues and tuition and which families still owe money. Such statements are usually filed during the periods when registration for the educational program is underway.

2. Date of checks or machine tapes totaling small checks that have been accepted for deposit.

3. Date of deposit of individual checks and checks recorded on the machine tape.

4. Sources of income. If the machine tape includes small checks for both tuition and dues, the total of checks for tuition should be recorded under the column headed tuition and the total of checks for dues recorded under the dues column. Other columns might include donations, laboratory fees in connection with the educational program, interest earned on savings deposits, and miscellaneous.

FIGURE 4

GIFTED CHILD SOCIETY

TREASURER'S REPORT

Attached are the statement of financial position as of February 12, 1974, the statement of expenditures and revenues for the priod January 1. January 31, 1974, the Ford Foundation Project statement, and the summary of expenditures and revenues for the fiscal year February, 1973 to January, 1974.

The Gifted Child Society holds a total of $21,682.03 of which $6,700.43 is in the checking account and the balance is held in interest bearing deposits.

During January the Society spent $3,691.37 (a substantial proportion, $2,966.78, for the Ford Foundation Project). The principal items of expense were for salaries and rent.

As of today, $3,752.72 of the funds from the Ford Foundation Project have been spent. The bulk has gone for salaries, $3,450.00.

During the fiscal year that ended in January 31, 1974, the Society expended $63,211.30 and had revenues of $69,437.45 for a net profit of $6,226.15. The fall session had expenses of $21,103.31 and revenues of $25,137.25 for a net profit of $4,033.94. This was coupled with the $350.45 net profit during the summer and $1,841.76 net profit during the spring.

Treasurer

February 12, 1974

These are the categories under disbursements:

1. Payee, the person or organization to whom the money is being paid.

2. The number of the organization check used to pay payees.

3. Date the bill was received.

4. Date payment was made.

5. The amount of the check being paid.

6. There should be columns where expenses can be categorized. The following columns are suggested: telephone, postage, school supplies, publications, equipment, teacher reimbursement (for expenses), rent, printing (including mimeograph), refund (tuition refunds for children who withdraw), advertising, travel, salaries, savings (not actually an expense), and miscellaneous.

The books should be kept up to date. A number of weeks should not be allowed to pass without recording income and disbursements. Entries should be made in ink, although totals for columns should be made in pencil at the bottom of each page and carried forward to the top of the next page.

Records that should be kept to verify the entries in the ledger include the following items:

Income. Adding machine tapes, registration records that include dues payments, and stubs that can be detached from checks.

Disbursements. Bills submitted for payment, receipts for out-of-pocket expenses, and cancelled checks.

Important to the sanity of the treasurer and the integrity of the books is an accurate and easily understandable registration record from the school coordinator. This record should show the names of children enrolled in the enrichment program, grouped by family, whether family dues have been paid, the total tuition charged each child, the amount of tuition paid, and lab fees paid. There also should be a column for refunds due. Tuition should be paid at the time of registration, so there should not be too much to note in the tuition due column.

Audits and Such

As already mentioned, the Internal Revenue Service requires an annual audited statement of income and disbursements. The statement is initially prepared by the treasurer and audited by a certified public accountant. The Society has been fortunate in having a CPA as a member and he has made the audits free of charge. If there is no CPA in your organization, it will be necessary to go outside and find one—and probably pay him.

An audit is simply a check of the organization's financial records by a qualified person other than the one who kept the records and prepared the statement. The auditor generally will comment on the quality of the treasurer's books and make recommendations for improving the record-keeping. If the treasurer has only a minimal amount of bookkeeping experience, the auditor's advice can be invaluable. Of course, there is no reason why the treasurer should wait for an annual audit to seek counsel. It is the smart treasurer who asks questions before something happens that either costs the organization money or costs the treasurer much time and energy.

Although the Society has never bonded any of its personnel, an organization starting out might do well to bond both its treasurer and the school coordinator. This protects the organization against any big, unintentional errors and also against intentional hanky-panky.

Also, we suggest that the treasurer's books and the school coordinator's records be double-checked at least twice a year by the president of the organization, a committee, or the executive director. You have to rely on the honesty of the individuals performing the jobs, but the officers and administrators do have an obligation to all who have paid their money to make sure the money is being recorded accurately.

Chapter 9

Choosing a Format for the Educational Program

"Research studies on special needs of the gifted and talented demonstrate the need for special programs," according to the U.S. Commissioner of Education in his report to Congress in 1971. He states further: "Contrary to widespread belief, these students cannot ordinarily excel without assistance. The relatively few gifted students who have had the advantage of special programs have shown remarkable improvements in self-understanding and in ability to relate well to others, as well as in improved academic and creative performance. The programs have not produced arrogant, selfish snobs. Special programs have extended a sense of reality, wholesome humility, self-respect, and respect for others. A good program for the gifted increases their involvements and interest in learning through the reduction of the irrelevant and redundant."

In the same report, experts on education for the gifted were asked to give their views on the nature of special programs for the gifted. Here are some of the points they made:

● Conventional and standardized curriculum requirements are unimportant to the gifted.

● "Rather than studying grade level content required of the total group, an open curriculum based on individual interests" is desirable.

● The gifted require a program that allows them self-management and decision-making ability.

● The gifted need opportunities to learn in depth.

• Whatever the educational program for gifted children, it must be flexible enough to cater to different learning styles. Among the gifted and the talented, one may find persons who respond and function rapidly, those who are deliberate and contemplative, those who are logical and direct, or those who are exploratory and circuitous. . . . Teaching the gifted does not comfortably permit standard rules of procedure.

• Program objectives include stimulation of individual interests, development of student initiative, development of self-acceptance, concept development, and recognition of the early ability to undertake complex learning tasks.

So you know what the objectives and goals of your educational program are. What mold or molds do you pour the program into? Through the years, the Gifted Child Society has tried or considered nearly all of the possible formats for an out-of-school educational program. In the next few pages we'll examine these various molds—or formats.

How About Field Trips?

The Society began with field trips exclusively. Children and their parents visited museums, historical sites, facilities at nearby colleges and universities, and local businesses and industries, particularly those with a research component. The field trips can be very instructive if properly arranged. For example, when taking gifted children to a museum of natural history, it will not be entirely sufficient to march them up and down the halls looking at exhibits. To make the trip worthwhile, arrangements should be made in advance to go behind the scenes to see exhibits being prepared and scientists at work. The children should be able to ask questions of someone in authority. If the trip is to a nearby industry, there should be more than a tour of facilities. Again, someone should be available to describe activities, to answer questions, and to allow children to work at a computer console or work at a simple experiment in the laboratory.

However valid field trips are, they are not enough to sustain an educational program. It is unlikely that a child will come to know a theory inside out by visiting someone else's research lab. And, after all, how can you visit an abstract concept? The Society, then, while it still values and includes field trips in the educational program, believes an organization has to go beyond such activities if it is going to adequately serve the needs of the children over a long period of time.

How About After-School Classes?

The Society rejected the idea of establishing its educational program after school on weekdays. These are the main reasons the Society doesn't favor this arrangement:

1. Children usually start school between eight and nine in the morning and finish between two and three in the afternoon. It's a long day of studying, reading, listening, and recitation. Even though the enrichment program is entirely different from what children get in school, it's still asking them to spend a lot of time in intellectual pursuits—especially the youngest children.

2. Most children, particularly when they reach the late elementary grades, have homework assigned by their public school teachers. This must be accomplished sometime after school, in the afternoon or evening.

3. Today's school and society offer children of all ages a wide range of after-school activities: sports, community recreation teams, clubs, Scouts, religious instruction, and private lessons in music and dance. It can be a strain on everybody—children, parents, and organization—to add enrichment courses to the already-full after-school schedule of activities.

4. If children have to come some distance to the educational program—and some of the Society's students live as far away as sixty miles—it's not possible to conduct an educational program in the time available. And guess who has to be home to get supper? Usually the same person who brings the child to the program.

If the public schools do offer special enrichment programs to gifted children, they are generally offered in the afternoon after school lets out. The public schools really have no choice. If they are going to provide special programs, they almost have to be after school and not on weekends when school is usually closed.

How About Saturday Workshops?

Whenever they have been questioned on the subject, parents in the Gifted Child Society have always opted for Saturday mornings as the best time to conduct an enrichment program. So, the Society has conducted its educational program on ten Saturday mornings each fall and spring since the early 1960s.

The Saturday morning schedule has many advantages:

1. It's easier to get teachers for Saturday morning classes than after school. Like the children they teach during the week, they're tired after a seven-hour day.

2. There are fewer conflicts with other activities on Saturday mornings.

3. Usually, both husband and wife are at home on Saturday morning. This can mean that: (a) one parent is available to drive the child to classes or get him to public transportation; (b) one parent is available to tend younger children at home while the other gets the gifted child to the program; (c) one or both parents are available to attend parent seminars, which are conducted at the same time classes meet.

4. If the organization's program is going to be conducted in a school building, which is likely, then there is probably a better chance to get the space on Saturday morning than after school.

Summertime, and the Livin' Is Busy

After a short stint with field trips and club activities, the Society started a summer session. There have been five-week summer sessions ever since, combined with the Saturday workshops. Although a summer session will be difficult or impossible to schedule in districts that have adopted a year-round schedule, in most districts it is possible and desirable. A summer session for gifted children fits naturally into the general pattern of today's summer school activities. Many public schools that used to run a summer session only for students who failed a subject during the regular school term, now offer courses students can take for enrichment or for the fun of it.

The Society conducts its summer session from late June to late July. Because schools in different parts of the country close and reopen at different times, local conditions and habits may dictate a different time period.

The Society's summer program operates every weekday, morning and afternoon. However, very young children attend mornings only. Even some older children choose to attend only half a day. Gifted children are still children, and there are other summertime fun activities attractive to children.

What About a Full-time Private School?

On and off for the last ten years, members of the Gifted Child Society have debated the merits of establishing a full-time private school instead of operating Saturday and summer workshops. There are two principal reasons why the Society has not attempted its own full-time school: (1) philosophically, the majority of officers and/or members support the public schools; (2) the capital costs are prohibitive. The philosophical opposition has been the main factor.

The last time the total membership was canvassed on the subject, of the thirty-four percent of questionnaires returned, fifty-seven percent of the respondents favored a full-time school, thirty-seven percent were opposed, and the remainder had either no opinion or didn't answer the question. When the same respondents were asked whether they would send their own children to a full-time school, fifty percent said yes.

A special committee studying the future direction of the Society looked at the results of the questionnaire and considered all aspects of the question. One thing the committee discovered was that most parents who favored a full-time school had very young children in the program. Parents of older children tended not to favor it. We came to the conclusion that the longer a child is in a public school, the more aware his parents are of the benefits of keeping him there. A gifted child is already different from other children because of his brightness. By isolating him in a closed environment, that difference becomes just that much more pronounced. Since the gifted child is going to have to live his life with all kinds of people, the committee reasoned, shouldn't he learn in school to get along with others?

In the end, the committee issued its recommendation to the executive board and membership, and the committee's report clearly reflected the majority's philosophy: "The majority of the committee decided that it would want to keep our workshop program in its present successful form, while making a strong effort to promote programs for bright and gifted children in the public school system. . . . " This is a goal also cited in the constitution and by-laws of the Society (Appendix B). It has always been our intention to eventually put ourselves out of business and have the public schools provide appropriate education for gifted students during the school week.

Here are some questions to raise within your own organization when you consider the matter of starting a full-time school:

1. Should gifted children be completely isolated from all other children?

2. Are the disadvantages—principally the estrangement from other children—outweighed by the advantage of having more time to offer a broader educational program?

3. Can financial backing for a private school be secured?

4. Are there enough parents willing to support the school by paying for their children to attend?

5. By operating a full-time school and charging more tuition than would be necessary for a part-time program, will many children who could profit from the program be denied the opportunities for enrichment?

The Gifted Child Society has chosen to sponsor Saturday workshops and a summer session instead of a full-time school for what it thinks are sound reasons. It wants. . .

• to offer enrichment and an opportunity for bright children to learn from exceptional teachers and other bright children.

• to enable children to remain in the mainstream of public education and experience a diverse society.

• to provide a teaching-learning model for gifted children which the public schools are encouraged to copy and include in their 180-day school year.

Chapter 10

Which Children Should Be Admitted?

In a limited way we've already talked about the criteria for admitting children (Chapter 4), but now we'll discuss the matter more fully. The first question to answer is, "What are you trying to do, and for whom are you doing it?" Suppose your organization wants to reach only the most gifted children for a full-time private school. Consequently, your group may decide to admit only children with an individually tested IQ score of 140 or over from a tri-county area. However, your organization may decide to offer a part-time enrichment program for as many children who can profit from it as possible. In that case, you will probably lower the IQ requirement, add other criteria, and open the program up to children in a smaller geographical area.

IQ as a Standard

IQ testing has come under sharp criticism in recent years. The attack generally has been made on three fronts: (1) present intelligence tests measure only how well white, middle-class people have learned or have the capacity to learn from a white, middle-class culture; (2) an IQ is not a static score, but can be increased if a person denied learning opportunities finally has been given them; (3) scores from group IQ tests often are not dependable. From what most experts in psychology and testing have said, there is some truth in all three arguments, perhaps to varying degrees.

It might be helpful to examine just what the intelligence test is designed to measure. Henry Chauncey and John E. Dobbin, test experts, described the aims of the intelligence test in their book *Testing: It's Place in Education Today* (New York: Harper & Row, 1963):

A significant point about all intelligence tests is that they measure only the individual's capacity for learning. No intelligence test opens a window in the student's skull through which psychologists can ascertain the amount of latent brightness or intelligence he has. A rough appraisal of the individual's comparative capacity for learning is the most that the best test of intelligence can provide.

... Even though "native intelligence" is suspected to exist, the intelligence tests we use in this generation measure not innate ability but a developed ability in which innate ability and learned behavior are mixed in unknown proportions.

Some experimental work has been accomplished in reducing the effects of environment on intelligence test performance. [But] all tests of intelligence used in our schools are used to predict success in our schools as they are.

[An] important characteristic of intelligence tests is that the estimates of learning capacity they provide are always comparative. That is, no intelligence test yields a measure of learning capacity or "intelligence" in absolute units like quarts or centimeters or ohms. Rather, the intelligence test ... only tells whether a particular student has done better or worse than a number of other students on the same learning jobs— and, within gross limits, how much better or worse.

With this in mind, what about using the intelligence quotient, the IQ or score, as a criterion for admitting children to your educational program? Your organization should consider these points:

• Intelligence tests do measure a child's capacity to learn what most educated people think is important to learn about our world. No matter how imperfect, they are still one of several good means of assessing that ability.

• The intelligence test designed to be administered to large groups of students throughout the country gives a comparative score.

The individual's score is based on how well others of his age and/or grade did on the same test. This is one reason why the IQ from a group test may be undependable. The organization that wants to cater to a very select group of the most gifted children probably should require each candidate for admission to be tested individually.

• The intelligence test score may tend to confirm or explain other observations and measurements of ability. In an early chapter we told about a child enrolled in the Society's program who had been labeled disruptive in the public school. Only after an individual intelligence test was administered was it possible to explain his behavior in terms of his being severely frustrated in learning.

Setting Other Criteria

Your organization may decide not to use an intelligence score at all as a criterion for admission to its educational program, or it may decide to use the IQ only in conjunction with other criteria. In either case, these guidelines might be helpful:

School recommendation. The recommendation from the school the child regularly attends could be the sole criterion for determining the eligibility of a child. The Society accepts a teacher recommendation exclusively for a scholarship application. (See fig. 3.) Every child enrolled in the Society's program must be recommended by his school's administrator, or by qualified testing personnel, as being mature and emotionally well adjusted and likely to benefit from an enrichment program (See fig. 5.) Pre-schoolers are individually tested. The school's recommendation most likely will be based on IQ, achievement testing, and perhaps just as important, the observations of the teacher.

Class standing. Your organization might choose to accept for admission to its educational program only those children in the upper five percent or ten percent of their class. Class standing is usually based mostly on achievement test scores and grades awarded. It is possible that a child can be in the upper ten percent of his class and not be gifted. If an IQ or a teacher's recommendation is used in addition, it can help identify the children most likely to need and benefit from an enrichment program.

Evidence of interest. When the Society first began, children who applied for the program were required to submit a brief essay describing their interests and how they might benefit from an enrichment program. What Society officials looked for in the essay was

Figure 5

ELIGIBILITY FORM

THE SATURDAY WORKSHOP

Sponsored by the Gifted Child Society, Inc.

Child's Name...

Address ....

Date of Birth...........................Grade...........Phone....................................

Dear School Administrator or Testing Personnel:

In order to participate in our program, a child must have an I.Q. of 120 or over, or have an I.Q. percentile of 92 or over.

Since we do not wish to damage confidence by placing a child into a group in which he cannot compete, we welcome your comments below.

The above child does........does not........satisfy the I.Q requirements.

He/she is..........is not..........mature and well adjusted from both discipline and emotional standpoints.

He/she would..........would not..........likely benefit from a program for above average children.

Our school does not have I.Q. records for this child...........................

Comments:

Since our program is a demonstration school, we request your assistance in providing the following statistical information:

TEST ADMINISTERED	SCORE	DATE
....	....	....
....	....	....
....	....	....

....
Signature & Title

....
Name & Address of School

....
Date

As is customary in demonstration schools, the media may show students in class. Submission of this form to the Gifted Child Society is understood to signify parental consent.

---

evidence of the student's broad interests, his ability to express himself, his desire to know more, and the creativity he demonstrated in constructing the essay. It is not a sufficient criterion by itself, but your organization may feel it has merit along with other criteria. After establishing the criteria for admission into the educational program, don't put them aside. Review them periodically, especially in the beginning years. Make sure they are suitable for the kind of program you are conducting or want to conduct. For most of its history the Society has debated raising its IQ standard from 120 and changing its criteria. The Society has been criticized from time to time for not raising the level, but the majority of members and officers have felt that 120 was adequate to attract children who could benefit from the programs offered. There have been very few instances in which children with IQ's of 120 have not been able to learn side by side with other children in the program.

Deciding Age Limits

Twelve years ago the Society offered courses for children between the ages of eight and fifteen. The minimum age is now four. Where should your organization start? The answer depends, of course, on what you're trying to do and for whom. Conceivably, a program could be designed and run just for gifted teenagers. Or there could be a program for gifted pre-kindergarten children only.

A good age bracket to being with is seven to ten, or children in grades two through five. The Society has always attracted more children between the ages of five and eight than from any other age span. Children in this range are lively and easy to teach. Even if school has been a bore for them, they are still young enough that their curiosity and free-wheeling inventiveness have not been stunted.

In any case, no one recommends starting with a program for children aged four to eighteen. There are some difficulties trying to reach children that are at opposite ends of this age spectrum. In order to design a good program for pre-kindergarten children, the organization must have teachers who are well prepared to work with young children. There may not be many such teachers available to you—a good reason to move slowly in that direction. One reason for not moving quickly into programs for gifted teenagers is that they are hard to attract and harder to hold. Many courses for teenagers don't get off the ground. When children are in middle and high school, they carry heavy academic loads and are actively engaged in other pursuits—including pursuit of the opposite sex. Some high school students also have jobs after school and on Saturdays.

Probably the best advice to give your organization is this: start with children in a fairly limited age range; it's easier to expand later.

Getting Information from Schools and Parents

We have already mentioned that it is desirable to have school recommendations for each child enrolled in your educational program. The eligibility form used by the Society is one way of getting information from the school. Through the years, the Society has found schools cooperative and prompt in completing eligibility forms and mailing them directly to the Society.

The eligibility and enrollment forms (fig. 5) are sent to parents after they apply to have their child enrolled. The eligibility form is then sent or hand-delivered by the parents to the principal of the school their child attends. The school sends the completed form to the Society. The enrollment form asks for vital statistics about the child and requests that the child and/or his parents select courses. Courses are selected from a brochure parents receive with the enrollment form. Brochures are issued prior to each Saturday workshop, and they will be discussed in more detail later in the book. A separate bulletin is issued prior to the summer session. The enrollment form will be considered again when we talk about registration procedures.

It is conceivable that an organization starting off with a very small educational program might want to conduct an interview with each child and his parents. Information may be obtained at such a session and organization officials may be able to make a first-hand assessment of the child's interest and abilities. Such a procedure is only possible where the program is very limited in the number of children enrolled, and where parents and children can make appointments for interviews at a time and place convenient to them and to organization registrars.

Chapter 11

Deciding What Courses to Offer

In the current Saturday workshops, the Society is offering more than fifty courses in different subject areas tailored to children of different ages and interests. It's quite an assortment. Through the years, hundreds of different courses have been offered. Some never got off the ground, some lasted one semester and were dropped, some lasted a year or two and were "rested," and some have been repeated year after year with great success. Naturally, the selection of courses is crucial to your educational program. If the courses are designed to attract and meet the needs of the children you're serving, you will do well. If the courses are poorly conceived, you will learn that quickly. Enrollment will dwindle to the point where the educational program and the organization itself may no longer exist.

What Do You Want to Happen for Children?

We have to say once again that the organization must be clear in the goals it sets for itself and for those it serves. In the case of determining what courses to offer, the organization has to consider not only what subjects would be most popular but also what subjects are necessary to give gifted children as many opportunities for development as possible and to prepare them for leadership roles and for living in a diversified society.

Also, the organization must decide whether it is going to provide enrichment only in academic subjects and in the creative arts, or whether it is also going to provide experiences designed to prepare children for careers. And what about recreation? Should the program include instruction and participation in games and sports?

The goals adopted by the organization generally depend on the size of the program planned and the availability of teachers, space, and eligible children. When the organization starts out, it will want to offer a limited number of courses. It would be unrealistic to adopt a program that gives children unlimited opportunities in all academic subjects, the arts, career preparation, and leadership training. But it is also unwise and unfair to children to start off with goals that fail to expand the organization's and children's horizons as the enrollment grows.

Who Makes the Decisions?

At the start, a curriculum committee composed of parent-educators should be primarily responsible for chosing courses and recommending them for approval and adoption by the executive board. Later on, the organization probably will want to hire a part-time curriculum coordinator to take charge of the planning and work in conjunction with the curriculum committee. The executive board should make the final determination based on recommendations from the coordinator and/or committee.

Where do ideas for courses come from? The reason for having educators on the curriculum committee is to draw on their experience and knowledge. But committee members and the curriculum coordinator shouldn't be the sole source of ideas for courses. Teachers employed by the organization to teach a particular course might come up with ideas for other courses they or someone else can teach. Other parents in the organization may have suggestions based on their own experience and that of their friends. Don't forget the children themselves. The Society's students suggest subjects for the educational program through their student council. Figure 6 is a form distributed to all children in Society workshops by the Student Advisory Council. The results of the survey are turned over to the curriculum committee after being interpreted by students in the computer class.

So, the curriculum committee and curriculum coordinator not only originate ideas for courses, they also screen the suggestions of others! Despite their dual role, they still must base their initial decisions on the established goals of the organization and its estimate of the availability of children for courses, teachers and space.

Whatever courses are eventually decided upon, they should have these factors in common:

Figure 6

TO: GCS Student Body

From: GCS Student Advisory Council

Re: New Courses

Please complete the following questionnaire today and return it to either your teacher or the main desk on the first floor.

Check the courses below that you would like to take. Pick as many as you wish so we know what we should recommend. Thank you.

Folk Dancing and Singing	Astrology
Journalism	History
Electronics	Rap Session
Advanced Computers	Ancient Peoples
Life in Other Countries	Psychology
Photography	Parapsychology
Book Reviewing	Meteorology
Speed Reading	Trivia
Writing	Advanced Art
Nature	Puppetry
Archeology	Drama
Science	Drug Abuse
Foreign Language	

What courses that do not appear above would you like to see offered? We would like your opinion listed below.

Would you attend student council meetings if they were held at 9:00 A.M. instead of 12:00 noon?   Yes   No

1. They should not duplicate instruction offered in the schools.

2. They should not restrict children to a certain number of tasks and goals. They need to be open-ended, allowing children to specialize and go in directions they might not have planned on at the start.

3. They should give children opportunities to make judgments, analyze, evaluate and form conclusions.

4. They should enable children as much as possible to make things, to take things apart and put them together, to experiment with things, to create and invent, and to express themselves.

5. They should be varied in nature. One of the drawbacks to public education is that most children are required most of the time to learn the same thing in the same away. Often the prescribed school course in physics requires all students to use the same workbooks, listen to the same lectures, and complete the same experiments. A special program for gifted children should offer physics in such a way that children can acquire and apply knowledge differently.

We spoke earlier of "resting" a course for awhile. It has been the Society's experience that some courses will draw very well for a year or two and then enrollment will drop off. Enrollment might decline for several reasons. If one teacher has been teaching the course for a couple of years, it's possible that he or she is losing the freshness and enthusiasm that made the course popular in the first place. Another reason could be that a lot of new and exciting courses have been added recently attracting children away from some of the older courses. Occasionally, children's and parent's interests change for no apparent reason other than as a response to a shift in emphases and societal concerns.

Science and More Science

The Society could offer only science courses and probably fill every empty classroom we could lay our hands on. We're not sure why there is such interest. Perhaps the passion for science is mostly an expression of society's priorities, or evidence of the special ability and interest of gifted children, or the result of the influence of the media, or parental pressure. Whatever it is, children want science from the time they're four years old.

The popularity of science is certainly due in part to the emphasis that society and the schools have placed on the subject, particularly since the late fifties. When the Russians sent Sputnik into space, the United States reacted by putting a lot of money into science and math. As a result, the National Defense Education Act pumped a lot of federal money into training science and math teachers to improve the quality of instruction in both subjects. A national thrust of such magnitude could hardly avoid affecting the interests of children and their parents.

One former curriculum coordinator has her own observations about why science courses are gobbled up. She believes that:

1. Science courses allow children to specialize at an early age, an opportunity usually not possible in the public schools in the elementary grades.

2. Science courses are do-it courses. There are experiments to perform, things to take apart and put together, rockets to build, and computers to program. Gifted children need these kinds of activities.

3. What students construct in science courses—electrical circuits, dinosaur dioramas, and so on—can be taken home. Parents of gifted children are parents. They're impressed by projects.

4. Many parents believe science and math courses will best prepare their children for a career.

5. In the Society's program even pre-school children can have an hour or more for science. This is unheard of in most public schools. Indeed, in the lower grades, many children don't get much more than an hour or two of science in one week. There are few, if any, opportunities to experiment and explore on an individual basis.

Through the years, the Society has tried to offer children of different ages and interests a variety of courses in physics, chemistry, botany, anatomy, and other sciences. Here is a sampling from a recent Saturday workshop:

• "Six-Legged Science." For children six and seven. A study of insects by means of filmstrips, stories, and live specimens.

• "Model Rocketry." For children seven and eight. Children learn the principles of space flight and rocket design and then construct and fly their own rockets.

• "The Space Lab." For children nine to eleven. An astronomy course that includes a field trip to a planetarium.

- "Animal Kingdom." For children five and six. An examination of everything from protozoa to vertebrates with particular attention paid to studying how animals adapt to their different environments.

- "Mini-Scientists." For children five and six. A study of such things as the rain cycle, the organs of the body, and electronic circuitry. Students are given the opportunity to build a terrarium, dissect organs and bones, and even devise a minicomputer.

- "The Human Body." For children six and seven. Learning what happens inside your body when you breathe, run, swallow, sleep, or have a stomach ache. Dissection of simple animal specimens is included.

- "Energy Crisis." For children six and seven. An examination of the origin and use of fuel, the alternatives to fossil fuels, and the effect of the energy crisis on the environment.

- "What Makes It Tick?" For children seven and eight. Learning how to systematically conduct and record experiments, using such devices as levers, wheels, and gears.

- "Now Science." For children seven and eight. A study of such present-day topics as pollution and sewage, space technology, radio astronomy, lasers, and computers.

- "Microbes—Friend and Foe." For children eight to ten. A course featuring individual investigation and actual bacteriological experimentation and a study of the causes and prevention of human disease.

- "Advanced Rocketry." For children nine and over. Exploration of rocket design, theory, and practice. Students will design rockets of their own and then test their design theories.

- "Your Project Is What?" For children nine and over. A very personalized course that enables students to pursue an area of science which interests them most.

- "Science and Other Things." For pre-schoolers four and five. Children study why objects sink or float, why it rains or snows, why the fur seal is becoming extinct, and why wood burns and stones do not.

- "The Great Outdoors." For children five and six. An introduction to the concept of ecology.

- "Dinosaur Dynasty." For children five and six. Studying and discussing dinosaurs by using filmstrips and slides, by making clay models, drawing pictures, and building dioramas.

- "All Kinds of Science." For children six and seven. Microscope slides are made and examined, chemical experiments are conducted, and "fossils" are made.

- "Over 200 Bones and 500 Muscles." For children six and seven. A basic study of the human anatomy.

- "Chemistry or Magic?" For children seven and eight. Lots of experimentation; a course that puts magic and logic into chemistry.

- "The Anatomy of a Hospital." For children seven to nine. Children study a modern hospital's operations by visiting a hospital and learning firsthand about such things as admitting procedures, intravenous feeding, contamination and sterilization, and electrocardiology.

- "Marine Biology." For children eight to ten. An examination of marine animal specimens, a study of the tides and currents, and of the animal and mineral treasures of the oceans.

- "Star Trek." For children eight to ten. A study of the universe, including a field trip to a planetarium.

- "More What Makes It Tick." For children nine to eleven. A chance for students to construct their own electric buzzers, motors, generators, and lenses.

- "Earth Exploration." For children six and seven. A study of the earth's rocks and minerals, with emphasis on how to use the earth's resources properly.

- "Physics with No Math." For children six and seven. Finding answers to such questions as: "How does water travel up to the third floor drinking fountain?" "Why is a gold bar heavy and a feather light?" "How is your arm like a steam shovel?"

- "Chemistry or Magic? II." For children nine to eleven. Less magic and more logic; more sophisticated experiments.

All the courses listed above are not taught at the same time. They are scheduled throughout the period beginning at 9 A.M. and ending at 1 P.M. It is obvious—but nevertheless worth pointing out—that the sciences are approached in a variety of ways to cater to children of different abilities and interests.

There are two other programs in the science field, both of them for students of junior and senior high school age. The first, the Hospital Seminar, takes place at a community hospital and actual hospital facilities are used. Staff specialists hold discussions and conduct visits to selected patient care areas. These include operating rooms, the emergency room, kitchen and housekeeping areas, and radiology and pathology laboratories. It is, in fact, a mini pre-med and paramedical course. The second program for older children includes both introductory and advanced studies in electronics at a nearby university.

The gifted child who is interested in math —anyone from the ordinarily curious child to the "math freak"—also can pick from among different courses. For example:

• "Introduction to Computers." For children nine to eleven. A study of such concepts as binary numbers, logic, flow charting, and computer programing. All students get the chance to spend time at a computer.

• "Whodunit." For children eight to ten. This is a course in logic.

• "The Numbers Game." For children seven and eight. An exploration of such topics as liquid measurement, geometric figures, linear measurement, the slide rule, and compass construction.

Abstract Concepts and the Arts

Humanities courses are popular after the children get into them. The problem is getting children into them. Some people believe that humanities must be offered at the very start of the educational program and that children should be led—almost pushed—into courses other than science and math.

How do you make courses in abstract concepts—creativity and the arts—attractive to children and their parents? Here are some guidelines that might help.

1. Allow all those who want to take science and math to select a science or math course as their first choice. These courses fill up quickly. When the children or their parents choose a second course, point out that science and math courses are full and recommend a course in the humanities or the arts.

2. As far as possible, make the courses in abstract concepts, writing and the arts. We mentioned that one reason for the popular-

ity of science and math courses is that there are experiments to perform and projects to work on. Don't make humanities courses strictly discussion courses.

3. If music instruction is offered, don't make it available to children older than seven or eight. By that age most interested children are taking private lessons.

This is a sampling of courses offered by the Society in concepts, writing, and the arts:

• "A Is for Art." For pre-schoolers four and five. Creating two and three dimensional projects from a multitude of media.

• "Children's Grab Bag." For children five and six. A course with a variety of activities designed to stimulate interest in science, art, music, social studies, and sensory perception.

• "Paint Pots, Puppets and Prints." For children six and seven. A course to stimulate visual awareness and the excitement of creating through printmaking and other art forms.

• "Great Stories from Great Music." For children seven and eight. An examination of favorite musical productions, including some acting and set design.

• "Get into the Act." For children seven and eight. Children learn to express themselves via pantomime, monologues, skits, and plays.

• "I Can't Believe I Wrote the Whole Thing!" For children eight to ten. Expression through free verse, short stories, and play writing.

• "Music for Young People." For pre-schoolers four and five. A chance to express rhythm and to sing, improvise, and learn about musical instruments.

• "Art for Young People." For children five and six. Features printmaking, sculpting, puppetry, and painting.

• "Fun with Music." For children five and six. Children not only listen to music, they also act it out.

• "Beginning Sculpture." For children six and seven. An opportunity to create in clay, paper, sand, and plaster.

• "Mini Music Makers." For children six and seven. Introduction to music theory and harmony; children have an opportunity to orchestrate for their own rhythm band.

• "Rap Session." For children nine and over. Suggested by the Student Advisory Council, this course gives children a chance to bring up almost any topic, from student rights to honesty in politics. The discussion leader shows children how opinions can be turned into constructive action.

• "So You Like to Argue." For children nine and over. A course to develop self-expression, thought and word processes, as well as to encourage the student to gain poise and self-assurance.

And Other Subjects

In a constant attempt to fulfill the ideal of the all-around gifted child, the Society offers courses that allow children to grow in different directions. Here are some of the courses:

• "Animated Films." For children nine and over. Using professional equipment, children make their own animated films—quite sophisticated stuff!

• "Chess—Theory and Practice." For children nine and over.

• "What's up, Doc?" For children five and six. Through pantomime, monologues, role playing, and simple filmmaking techniques, children make comic strip and movie cartoon characters come alive.

• "Festivals, Fiestas, and Fireworks." For children six and seven. Sociology and anthropology taught by studying important holidays in different countries.

• "It's Magic." For children seven and eight. Developing new tricks and learning old ones.

• "Read All About It!" For children eight to ten. An introduction to journalism and a chance to produce the Saturday workshop newspaper.

• "The Wide World of Sports." For children nine to eleven. A way to learn about teamwork, leadership, sportsmanship, fair play, and competition through a study of different sports.

In most of these courses children are learning either concepts or values as they engage in fun activities. For example, it was hoped that children would learn a lot about human behavior by taking "Wide World of Sports." One always hears that varsity sports in high school teach sportsmanship and fair play, but this is not always so. Many coaches assume these values will rub off, but they may not.

In this course, the values were uppermost. During the summer session, when many children spend the whole day in the program, there are games and sports activities strictly for fun and exercise.

In past years the Society has offered a course in study skills. It was very popular with children and parents. Most children, whether they're gifted or not, are not taught all they need to know about independent study, library research, and report preparation. For the gifted child the lack of such knowledge can be particularly frustrating. The gifted child is ready to undertake independent study and research at an earlier age, and this interest can be blunted if he has not learned how to study. Unfortunately, gifted children often are not given the chance to take a study skills course because it is assumed they know everything there is to know about studying. Your organization might consider offering study skills in its first batch of courses.

Going on Safari

Field trips are a part of many courses given at the Society's Saturday workshops and during the summer session. But the granddaddy of all field trips is called the Traveling Classroom Safari. The safari is a one-week trip for children seven and over, and it is scheduled for the last week of the five-week summer session. Some of recent safaris have included:

• A two-state bus trip to Mark Twain's home, the Baseball Hall of Fame at Cooperstown, New York, glassworks, a coal mine, and the Valley Forge encampment site.

• A tour of Cape Cod, Massachusetts, that included visits to such places as the Wellfleet Bay Wildlife Sanctuary, the Sealand Marine Aquarium, and the Cape Cod Museum of Natural History, with side trips to Boston and historic Sturbridge Village.

• A trip to the Adirondacks wilderness in New York State and Canada.

But the safari is not just a tour or a fun trip. The summer program director made this point with parents in a bulletin about the summer program: "The safari is not simply a tour, but rather a culmination of related studies dealing with places to be visited. The fun, the challenge, the learning, and the acceptance of responsibility— away from home for the first time perhaps—all represent real giant steps which could not be duplicated by any book reading or classroom experience."

Much of the curriculum during the four weeks preceding the safari is preparation for the trip. Prior to the trip to the Adirondacks and Canada, the children engaged in these studies:

Science. Children investigated the St. Lawrence Seaway and examined the problems of ecology and land use affecting both Canada and the United States.

Humanities. Children studied the interdependence of the peoples of the world and the separate philosophic and economic problems that must be met by global cooperation.

Through the years the teachers and students in the Society's courses have been free to do a lot of things they wouldn't have been able to do in the public schools. They did things—like team teaching— long before the public schools discovered it was a good idea. Children seven to fifteen have worked together in a drama production class; older children and pre-schoolers teamed together to study current events; in a discussion class, children have invited a "guest" friend or relative to take part; and the creative arts class made musical instruments for a music class. So it has gone and so it continues.

Chapter 12

Finding, Guiding, and Keeping the Right Teachers

Just because this chapter follows the chapter on course design, we don't mean to imply that all courses must be conceived before the teachers are hired. We've mentioned that teachers hired by the organization often can be instrumental in suggesting courses to offer. Indeed, the organization may go after a particularly fine teacher of science and then ask him or her to suggest possible courses to teach.

Who Makes a Good Teacher of the Gifted?

Not enough colleges or universities train teachers of the gifted. Your organization, therefore, may not come upon people trained in "teaching the gifted." For that matter, you may not find teachers with much, if any, experience in filling the special needs of gifted children. Incidentally, when looking for teachers, don't assume that advanced degrees and years of teaching experience automatically spell q-u-a-l-i-t-y. Listed below are some of the qualities and traits the Gifted Child Society looks for in a teacher:

1. Knowledge of the field. The teacher should be expert in the subject he's going to teach—whether it's electronics or magic. The person whose knowledge is shallow will be no match for the inquisitive minds of gifted children.

2. Creativity. A teacher of gifted children has to be extremely inventive. He or she must come up with teaching methods, experiments, and projects that are different from those the children have done before.

3. Intelligence. The teacher does not have to be gifted, but he or she should be alert and open to new ideas.

4. Flexibility. Gifted children can wreak havoc with a carefully prepared lesson plan. The teacher has to be ready to move in new directions at the drop of an idea or a question.

5. Security. The teacher who feels insecure among gifted children will wear that insecurity like a red and yellow striped coat. If a teacher feels threatened or intimidated by students, he or she probably will never be able to work with them.

6. Enthusiasm. A teacher who is not really excited about working with gifted children will not excite his or her students.

7. Humanity. The person you're looking for has to like children. He or she should be able to display emotions naturally and be accessible to his or her students.

Using Professionals to Find Professionals

If you've taken to heart what we've said already, your organization will have professional educators in some leadership positions and on the curriculum committee. The educators on the curriculum committee also will be parents of children in the educational program. It's possible that some of the parent-educators are themselves good candidates for faculty positions. But if they aren't candidates for some reason, they certainly should be able to recommend some teachers in their own or other schools who fill the bill.

Your own staff members may be able to recommend likely candidates. Among teachers, there is usually agreement about who the outstanding teachers are.

In the early 1960s, when the Gifted Child Society was on the verge of expanding, our president at the time looked to his own regional secondary school system for teachers. He had developed programs for the gifted in his own system and hired teachers for these programs. He was able to identify a few who could do well with younger gifted children.

If your organization has no parent-educators, another way to use the professional judgment of educators is to have parents approach the principal or superintendent of their school and ask him or her to name one or two teachers that would do especially well with gifted children. Of course, the administrator has to be committed to helping gifted children. Otherwise, he or she may not be much help.

While it is extremely valuable to have educators picking fellow educators, parents also can be very helpful. The teacher who has been with the Society the longest time was originally suggested by parents who knew of his ability. Parents of gifted children who listen to their children talk excitedly about what a teacher has done for them in school probably can be sure that the teacher has something to offer gifted children.

Don't Forget the Non-Teacher Teacher

Perhaps one of the reasons why the public schools have never taken advantage of the wealth of talent in their community is because the profession is so adamant about requiring teachers to have proper certification. We have no quarrel with overall state policies requiring the licensing of teachers, but we do think non-certified people should not be automatically forbidden to teach. There should be provisions for allowing non-certified personnel to teach if they have experience and ability in a special field and if they like children. Fortunately, the private organization does not have to abide by regulations that make it difficult for the public schools to use a non-teacher as a teacher.

Over the years some of the Society's very best teachers have been non-teachers. That is, they have not been professional educators and have not been formally certified to teach. We are not referring to a mother or father who visits a class to show slides or to display a collection, we are speaking of laymen having *full charge* of a course.

Most recently, chess and magic have been taught by lay experts. There are no professional teachers licensed to teach chess and magic anyway! The Society also has employed laymen, including parents of children in the program, to teach science and arts courses. For example, a civil engineer turned out to be a real genius in the classroom. He not only knew physics and its applications, but he was extremely inventive in the techniques he came up with to help children learn. A member who worked for a box manufacturer turned out to be a whiz as a teacher of art. A systems analyst did a fine job teaching a science course.

The hospital course for older children—probably unique in the country—could not be taught in the classroom by a professional educator as well as it could be taught by the professionals in a hospital. And the Society has asked people in various fields to come to class and speak with the children about their profession and answer questions.

By the way, there has never been any jealousy between professional educators and non-professional educators on the Society's faculty. Everyone knows a pro when he or she sees one.

What to Pay Teachers

If your organization operates a part-time educational program similar to that of the Gifted Child Society, it will never attract teachers because of the salary paid. Let's face it, nobody's going to get rich by working fifty to one-hundred hours a year with gifted children. If your organization decides to operate a full-time school, then the salary scale will have to be competitive with those of other private schools.

There are several ways your group might decide what is a fair salary to pay part-time teachers:

1. Find out the average salary paid to public school teachers in your area. Then figure out what the pay would be on a hourly basis.

2. Determine the hourly wage paid an experienced substitute teacher.

3. Ask a professional educator on your executive board or board of trustees what he thinks a fair salary would be.

4. Find out what teachers are getting for other out-of-school activities and pay a little more than that.

The Society now has a faculty of almost forty teachers for its Saturday workshops. Many of them have at least a master's degree and many have tenure as public school teachers. The Gifted Child Society pays a teacher seventeen dollars an hour for the first two years and eighteen dollars an hour thereafter.

Getting It All Together

All right, your organization has determined the kind of teacher it wants, the number it wants and for what subjects, and the salary it will pay. Teachers who seem to fit the bill have been suggested. Now what?

As a small organization starting out, you might want to have members of the curriculum committee personally interview each prospective teacher. The interviews probably can be scheduled on two or three nights. If you proceed this way, don't overpower a candidate by having half a dozen committee members interview him. Two committee members might work together as an interviewing team, but three definitely would be a crowd. One team doesn't have to interview all candidates.

The curriculum coordinator for the Society does most of the interviewing now. All teacher candidates have been highly recommended by other teachers, parents, or outside experts. The Society has never advertised for teachers. Candidates, therefore, don't usually come to the Society. The coordinator tries to hire teachers the semester before they are to teach. That is, if he's looking for a science teacher for the spring, he tries to hire him in the fall. The teacher is then invited to observe fall workshop science classes. The coordinator and members of the curriculum committee are likely to be on hand to meet and evaluate the candidate. Members of the curriculum committee may also observe the teacher at work in his full-time job.

In his interview the coordinator tells the candidate something about the Society and its program. He mentions the course the candidate might teach but does not describe in any detail what the course is all about nor how it should be taught. That's what the Society is hiring the teacher to determine. The coordinator may say to a prospective teacher that a science course next spring for children aged seven and eight is tentatively titled "Sizzle and Brr." The course should present various aspects of heat and cold. The teacher might want to mix in a little meteorology, physics, and chemistry. Then ask the candidate, "What do you think you might do with the course?" The coordinator can tell a great deal about the teacher's qualifications by his response. If he replies by saying that the subject is too vague and couldn't possibly be taught to eight year olds, then the coordinator knows he has to look further. On the other hand, the teacher might respond, "Hey, I could have the kids make their own thermometers, and we could do some experiments to see how heat and cold affect different chemicals, and . . ." Then the coordinator is pretty sure he's got a live one.

The prospective teacher is asked to send a résumé. The coordinator usually goes over the résumé with the educator who recommended the teacher or with the teacher's superior where he is employed full-time.

When the Society decides to hire a teacher, two copies of a simple contract are mailed to the candidate. (See fig. 7 for the employee contract used for the Saturday workshops and fig. 8 for the summer session contract.) The Society found from experience that it is necessary to include a cancellation clause. Once in an early summer session an insufficient number of children enrolled, but the teacher contracts didn't give the Society any way out. The parents and children might have liked the very small student-teacher ratio, but the cost to the Society was excessive.

While on the subject of teacher-student ratio, it should be noted that very small class size is not always desirable. The Society has discovered that at least ten children are needed to begin a decent discussion and to sustain it. Even in science courses it's desirable to have enough children doing experiments so results can be discussed and shared.

The Society employs some teacher assistants, or aides. They are generally high school students. Many of them are graduates of the Society's program. These assistants are invaluable to the program. They help children with projects and experiments, escort younger children from class to class, help clean up after class, and share in the mothering and fathering of pre-schoolers. The same hiring procedures should be followed as with teachers. The Society pays aides two dollars an hour.

Before a person begins to teach, he or she is sent some general guidelines, curriculum forms for an outline of lesson plans, and a reimbursement form to cover any out-of-pocket expenses. (See Appendix E.)

Your organization should schedule an orientation meeting for teachers before each session of the educational program. Such meetings can be relatively informal, but it is helpful to have someone explain the way things usually happen during a session of the program. Teachers who have been with the group for a while can help new faculty members. An obvious advantage of getting together is to give the teachers an opportunity to meet each other before the term begins. It's rough on a new teacher if he or she has to come to the first day of the session as a stranger.

A new teacher in the Society's workshops is never scheduled for more than one course. The Society doesn't want him or her to be overwhelmed the first time out. And if the teacher turns out to be only second best, it's better to have a "second best" in only one course.

Figure 7

EMPLOYMENT CONTRACT

THE SATURDAY WORKSHOPS
Sponsored by the Gifted Child Society, Inc.

Date...

It is agreed between The Gifted Child Society, Inc., and...............
....that the Gifted Child Society, Inc., does
hereby employ him/her as a teacher/assistant in the Saturday Work-
shops, at the Travell Wing of the Benjamin Franklin Jr. High School
in Ridgewood, N.J.

Such employment shall be for ten Saturdays, from.......................
........................to..inclusive. School will be
closed on.. .
Course(s) to be taught will be:

   1. ....

   2. ....

   from........................ AM to................................. AM/PM
   in Room(s)...

Salary for above services will be in the amount of $.......................
payable in full after completion of the Workshops.

The Gifted Child Society reserves the right to rescind this contract if there is insufficient enrollment for the above courses. Should
the course(s) be cancelled, you will be notified no later than...............
....

Social Security Number..

....
                                   Curriculum Coordinator

....
                                   President

....
                                   Employee

Figure 8

GIFTED CHILD SOCIETY, INC.

Employment Contract

Date:......................................

It is agreed between the Gifted Child Society, Inc., and.......................
....that the Gifted Child Society does hereby employ him/her as instructor/teacher aide in the Summer Workshops held at the Travele Wing of the Benjamin Franklin Junior High School in Ridgewood, New Jersey.

Such employment shall be weekdays from June 28th to July 28th, 1972, inclusive, from 8:30 A.M. to 1:00 P.M. with the exception of additional times allotted to staff meetings, field trips and the overnight "Safari."

The instructor/teacher aide will............will not............be involved with the "Safari," beginning Monday, July 24th, and ending Thursday, July 27th, 1972.

The instructor of the younger group will be responsible for the complete supervision and coordination of one field trip.

The instructor/teacher aide of the older group will assume responsibility for overnight supervision according to the schedule arranged by the director.

Salary for the above will be in the amount of $...................................... . payable in full on July 28th, 1972.

If involved in the "Extended Day" activity for the older group until 3:00 P.M., additional salary will be $...................... per hour of afternoon activity.

The above contract shall be null and void if, due to insufficient enrollment, by June 15th, cancellation of a particular class becomes necessary. Notification will be made no later than June 21st.

DIRECTOR ....

PRESIDENT ....

EMPLOYEE ....

Lesson Plans Are for Changing

All Society teachers—new and experienced—are required to file lesson plan outlines for each course session prior to the beginning of a workshop. (See Appendix E and the completed lesson plans in Part II.)

The lesson plan outlines are not intended to lock a teacher into an inflexible program, they are used for three reasons:

1. After making a course outline, the teacher should come up with many creative ideas and projects. He also can plot a direction for the course—when to introduce a concept so that it prepares the children for something that will be taught later. And the teacher can see from his outline what kinds of materials and equipment he will need—and when he will need them.

2. The outline confirms for the organization that the teacher has creative ideas and knows how to make them pay off for children.

3. The curriculum coordinator can spot duplication of materials or activities within a course or between courses. Also, a review of the outlines can alert the coordinator to possibilities for joint class projects, team teaching opportunities, and ways for one class to do something for another class. Children in a drama class can read the writing of youngsters in a creative writing class.

But the lesson plan outlines are just that—outlines. There is no syllabus to follow come hell or high water. We've already said that the teacher of a gifted child has to be flexible and inventive. If your teachers are both, they are probably going to have to revise their preliminary outlines as they go along.

The teacher who is working with gifted children for the first time may be surprised to find out that he or she hasn't scheduled nearly enough activities or theories and concepts to be explored. The teacher who is accustomed to the usual public school classroom pace may be startled by the speed with which gifted children zip through materials, exhaust the ramifications of a problem, or come up with more and different answers than expected. A new math or science teacher may plan to spend the first period exploring a couple of abstract theories, and before the period is half over, the children have not only explored the two theories but several others that were scheduled for lessons two and three.

That is one way in which lesson plans will be revised or thrown out.

Here's another way. In the first session or two, teacher and students discover they're really into something they hadn't foreseen. A discussion has expanded into a series of fascinating projects. An exploration has led much farther than anyone expected, and the new direction appears to be far more exciting and educational than the one previously decided on. There go lesson plans three through ten.

Evaluating Teacher Performance

New teachers are observed at least three times by three different observers on three different Saturdays during a ten-week Saturday workshop. Experienced teachers are observed once or twice. In the early days of the Society's program, evaluations were not discussed with the teacher. That policy has been changed, and the Society strongly recommends that evaluations be discussed with the teachers on an individual basis.

Certainly they have a right to know what others have observed and the organization certainly has an interest in bringing to the teacher's attention what can be done to make the courses more profitable for the children.

All observations are conducted by professional educators who are members of the Society's curriculum committee and the curriculum coordinator. For the beginning organization without a curriculum coordinator, members of the curriculum committee alone will undertake the evaluation.

The Society has developed a simple observation form (fig. 9) for use by evaluators. You will notice that there is nothing on the form to indicate the teacher's appearance, voice quality, mannerisms or facial expressions. These observations detract from the primary objective for evaluation: Are the children learning from this teacher?

In the typical public school classroom, 60 to 70 percent of the class period may be taken up by the teacher lecturing. Observers of teachers of gifted children should expect to find very little of that. There should be a great deal of interaction between students and teacher and among students. The important thing is whether learning is taking place in the room. The rest is trimming.

Figure 9

GIFTED CHILD SOCIETY

OBSERVATION FORM

Teacher... Course.................................

Room.................................... Time......................................

1. Do the children seem to want to be in this room?

2. Does the teacher show evidence of a give and take with students?

3. Does every child seem interested and actively involved?

4. Does the teacher talk on or near the children's level?

above

below

5. Are student responses natural or strained?

6. Is discipline lacking, controlled, or severe? Or is class and individual interest at such a high level that discipline is unnecessary and irrelevant?

7. Is there a diversity of materials and methods by which presentation is made?

8. Is there evidence of genuine creativity in this teacher's work?

9. Were you at any time caught up in the lesson to the point that you forgot this form?

10. Additional comments:

Class observed by...Date........................

The evaluator looks for activities that allow children to learn by seeing, touching, and smelling, and he or she is anxious to see if the teacher uses different approaches to get ideas across. In a public school a science teacher may show a film on insects for ten or fifteen minutes and then ask the class to discuss the film for the remainder of the period. Not good enough for gifted children! The teacher should have some live insects to be examined, some specimens to be dissected, and perhaps some specimens to be examined under a microscope. Off in a corner of the room, some children might be taking their own close-up pictures of insects.

The curriculum committee and coordinator also are guided in their assessment of a teacher by what they hear from parents and students. From time to time in recent years members of the Society's Student Advisory Council have observed teachers and filed critiques, but it's often not necessary to have formal observations from parents and children. Their informal evaluations are generally just as beneficial.

Sometimes it's possible to tell how great a teacher is by watching and listening to children coming out of his class. If they're excited, the chances are they have been turned on by a gifted teacher. Often our children come bursting into the workshop at full speed and leave slowly and reluctantly. But just because children are not on fire does not mean that their teacher is not effective. After all the years of observing teachers and learning, we still find it hard to come up with a definition of the perfect teacher. Teachers teach in different ways, just as children learn in different ways.

If most children in a class seem uninspired by what's happening in the course, the teacher is not likely to stay around long. If only one or two children seem turned off by a teacher, it may not be the teacher's fault, but in any event, the curriculum committee will evaluate the teacher again. If the teacher checks out, the children may be encouraged to enroll in another course.

Parents are listened to. Every Saturday workshop morning there are usually some members of the curriculum committee and officers on hand. Parents are encouraged to talk to them about any questions, suggestions and complaints Naturally, some of the parent's remarks will have to do with teachers and their performance. Such comments are weighed along with the comments of evaluators.

Chapter 13

Scheduling Teachers and Learning

Getting children and teachers together at the right times and in the right places is no easy task. Some public school districts have tried to make it easier by scheduling classes through a computer. It's not likely that your organization will be scheduling its educational program by computer. So, what's going to make the job easier for you? We hope this chapter will help.

Wanted: Person Who Is Inventive, Patient, and Flexible

Scheduling headaches are fewer when a competent person coordinates registration and sees that the educational program runs with a minimum of trouble. That person in the Gifted Child Society is the school coordinator. We mentioned before that your organization would be well served if it hired a part-time school coordinator very early in the life of its educational program. We call this to your attention again.

The Society's first two school coordinators were parents of children in the program. The third and current coordinator was hired when the Society advertised the position. Though the advertisement wasn't worded exactly like the heading above, it could have been. The want ad also might have called for someone who wouldn't give a second thought to dedicating her time, energy and dining room table to the cause of the organization for five or six weeks at a stretch.

The Society's coordinator has a bachelor's degree and has worked as a volunteer in several educational programs. She answered the

96

Society's ad because she was looking for a part-time job and because she had experience as the head of a parent tutorial project in her home town. Like the two school coordinators before her, she had no special training as a registrar or coordinator of school operations. But she is inventive, patient, and flexible. She has to be.

For about five weeks prior to each workshop, she and her family have to put with registration bedlam. Her home becomes the nerve center of the Society and her dining room table is the strategy and planning board.

The phone rings from 7 A.M. until midnight many days. The coordinator, however, does have help. A high school student works afternoons with her during the days preceeding a workshop. It's a good part-time job for a teenager who types labels, does filing, sometimes answers the phone, and answers the hundreds of requests for workshop brochures.

A school coordinator can't get through her work if she is easily flustered or abrasive. Her fortitude and stability are severely and continuously tested: an emotional mother calls to plead for her child who has been turned down because he did not meet entrance criteria; children by the score must be shifted from one class to another because of over-registration in several courses; a mother wants to enroll her six-year-old in four morning courses, something the Society won't sanction; parents who live too far away have to be discouraged from registering their child, because it would mean leaving their home at 6 A.M.

Programming for Individuals—Students and Teachers

The registration cycle for the Society's workshops begins in a number of ways:

• Parents whose children were enrolled in a workshop the previous semester may re-enroll their children for new courses.

• Parents are referred to the program by friends who have sent their children.

• A school principal, teacher, or psychologist suggests to parents that they enroll their child in the program.

• Parents read an advertisement or article about an upcoming workshop in a newspaper.

• Parents see the workshop brochure at a public library. (The Society sends brochures to libraries before every workshop session.)

Those parents who do not have a brochure call or write for one. The brochure lists all courses, describes their general goals and activities, and states what age groups are eligible, who the instructors are, and what time courses are given. The brochure also gives a thumbnail sketch of each instructor and all other necessary information about the Society and its program. At the same time the Society sends parents a brochure, it sends an eligibility form (fig. 5) which the parents must have completed by their child's school principal.

The brochure contains an enrollment form (fig. 10) and a membership form (fig. 11). Both forms are to be completed and returned to the coordinator. Parents must pay tuition at the time of registration and they must be paid-up members of the Society. We will discuss tuition later in this chapter.

Figure 10

ENROLLMENT FORM

SATURDAY WORKSHOP ● SPRING SEMESTER
REGISTRATION CLOSES MARCH 1st. CLASSES START MARCH 8th
ONE FORM PER CHILD — PLEASE DUPLICATE IF NECESSARY

CHILD'S NAME..
                                                                                    FIRST

ADDRESS ....
                                                        STREET

....
            CITY   STATE   ZIP   TELEPHONE

PREVIOUS WORKSHOP EXPERIENCE:

YES.................. NO..................

AGE........... GRADE........... B'DAY.. YES.................. NO..................
                                        MO.   DAY   YR.

IN CASE OF
EMERGENCY CONTACT...TELEPHONE:...............................

COURSE **DESIRED**	**KEY NO.**	**LAB FEE**	**ALTERNATE** **CHOICE**	**KEY NO.**	**LAB FEE**
9:00 A.M.			9:00 A.M.		
10:00 A.M.			10:00 A.M.		
11:00 A.M.			11:00 A.M.		
12:00 Noon			12:00 Noon		

TUITION CALCULATION
(COMPLETE ONLY **ONCE** PER FAMILY)

FIND NO. OF COURSES IN FAMILY
AND ENTER TUITION AT RIGHT

COURSES	TUITION	COURSES	TUITION
1	$30.00	4	$108.00
2	58.00	5	132.00
3	84.00	6	156.00

PLUS $24.00 PER ADDITIONAL COURSE

FAMILY MEMBERSHIP $8.00 $......................
(If not paid fall 1974)
TUITION $......................
ADD $15.00 FOR EACH 1½ HR. COURSE $......................
LAB FEES $......................
**CONTRIBUTIONS $......................
TOTAL ENCLOSED $......................
**(Tax deductible under Sec. 170 I.R. Code)

PLEASE MAKE CHECK PAYABLE TO GIFTED CHILD SOCIETY AND MAIL TO SCHOOL
COORDINATOR.

Figure 11

GIFTED CHILD SOCIETY, INC.

MEMBERSHIP FORM

MEMBERSHIP IN THE SOCIETY:

DUES PAID ....

OR DUES ENCLOSED...

MAILING LIST — PLEASE COMPLETE EACH TERM

FAMILY NAME...
                     LAST   HUSBAND   WIFE

ADDRESS ....
                            STREET

....
        CITY   STATE   ZIP   TELEPHONE

PROFESSION:

    HUSBAND ....

    WIFE ....

SPECIAL ABILITIES, HOBBIES, ETC.

    HUSBAND ....

    WIFE ....

The Gifted Child Society is a non-profit cooperative organization. Participation of both parents is needed. Growth of the Society has been achieved through active participation by members.

I THINK I CAN HELP BY..

I AM WILLING TO WORK ON THE FOLLOWING COMMITTEE:

☐ Community Action	☐ Membership Participation	☐ Research
☐ Curriculum	☐ Newsletter	☐ Saturday Workshop Activities
☐ Hospitality	☐ Phone Squad in my Area	☐ Scholarship
☐ Information Clearinghouse	☐ Planning and Finance	☐ Typing
☐ Legislative Action	☐ Program	☐ Ways and Means
☐ Library	☐ Publicity	☐ Where Needed
☐ Mailing		

We will contact you when commitee openings become available. Thank you for your offer of help.

The coordinator has three standard postcards she uses to communicate with parents during the registration period. One card thanks parents for returning the enrollment form, but informs them that the Society has not yet received the eligibility form from the school. The other card informs the parent that the Society has received the eligibility form from the school but not the enrollment form from them.

Standard postcards like these save the school coordinator a great deal of time. To complete the registration cycle, a third standard postcard is sent parents which confirms registration. In some cases refunds have to be made. A refund might be due if parents have paid in advance for three courses and their child can be registered for only two.

It should be pointed out that not all children who apply are accepted. In some cases the public school reports on the eligibility form that the child does not meet entrance requirements. In these instances the Society sends a letter to the parents (fig. 12) informing them of the school's report. The door may not be quite closed, however. The Society encourages parents to have their child individually tested if the group IQ score is five points or less short of the 120 cutoff. If the results of such an individual test indicate that the child meets the criteria, the parents may reapply.

We said earlier that a lot goes on between the time the eligibility and enrollment forms are received and the time the coordinator sends out the confirmation postcard. All kinds of juggling, persuading, advising, revising, and more juggling is what goes on. This is how it could happen:

Mr. and Mrs. Giff wish to enroll their six-year-old son Ted in the Society's workshop. All the necessary forms have been received and are satisfactory. The enrollment form requests Ted be enrolled in "Six-Legged Science" at 9 A.M. and "The Human Body" at 10 A.M.

By the time the Giffs send their enrollment form, "Six-Legged Science" is full. In fact the coordinator has squeezed an extra child into the class with the teacher's permission and has turned down two dozen other children. Another problem presented by the Giffs' form is that they have registered Ted for two science courses. This is Ted's first time at the workshop and the Society does not like to schedule anybody as young and new as Ted for two heavy academic courses.

Figure 12

The Saturday Workshops

Sponsored by the Gifted Child Society, Inc.

            RE:..

Dear

Thank you for your interest in our Saturday Workshops.

As you know, the requirement of the Society is that a child have an I.Q. of 120 or more, or an I.Q. percentile of 92 or over. On this basis, according to the report received, your child does not qualify for participation in the Saturday Workshops.

If you wish, you may have your child re-tested by a psychologist or testing agency of your choice. Please feel free to discuss this matter at any time with our school coordinator or executive director.

                    Sincerely yours,

                    President, Gifted Child Society

Membership check returned

Enrollment fee returned

Date:....................................

The coordinator calls Mrs. Giff to explain the situation: Ted can't get in "Six-Legged Science" but he can enroll in "The Human Body." Mrs. Giff goes along. The coordinator also suggests a "lighter" course in the arts—something where Ted can move around and have a change of pace. The Giffs accept this suggestion, too.

That's a simple case. It can get really hairy when a family has two children to enroll in a workshop with each child trying to get into two courses, and most are already full. Here are some other things the coordinator accomplishes:

• In order to take care of all the children who want a particular course, a duplicate section might be scheduled.

• Similar courses or different sections of the same course may be scheduled at different hours. A child who lives forty miles from the workshop site wants to take the course at 11 A.M. but the 11 A.M. course is full. The coordinator finds that a child who lives nearby is scheduled for the course at 11 and asks if he will switch to 9 A.M.

• More and more girls are taking science and math courses than ever before. But suppose by the time registration is nearly complete there is only one seven-year-old girl in a class. The coordinator calls the girl's mother and explains this fact, saying the Society has no objection but the little girl might feel uncomfortable. Very often in such situations mother and daughter agree. If they don't, that's all right, too.

• A child is scheduled for more than one science course in a row. One of the courses is full. The coordinator calls the parents to explain and suggests a humanities course that's open, or perhaps a class in music, art, or drama.

Parents have been very cooperative. If they are asked to switch their children from one class to another, nine times out of ten they will.

For every child in the workshop there is a 3 by 5 index card and a file folder. The card lists all courses taken by the child, the telephone number to be called in case of emergency, and information on family membership status. The card is maintained as long as the child continues attending workshops. The file folder contains the eligibility form, end of semester reports and comments, registration forms, and any other important information about the child. The folder comes in handy if a teacher is having difficulties with a child in class. He or she can look at the file to see if the child's school teachers or former workshop teachers made any comments that might shed light on the current situation.

The coordinator makes a list of students for each class. A copy goes to the teacher, a copy goes to the school committee chairperson, and the other goes into the file. Particularly in these days of the energy crunch, it is important to know what the chairperson of the school committee does with her copy. She tries to arrange car pools for those parents who are unable to transport their children to the workshop.

How Many Courses and How Long?

Very young children and those just starting in the Society's workshop are not permitted to take more than one course. Children are exposed to education in some form all week and perhaps also to a lot of outside activities as well. Children—even gifted ones—can handle just so much. As children grow older and demonstrate their capacity for enrichment, they are able to take more courses. But the Society never allows any child to take four courses in a row.

Most of the Society's workshop courses are an hour long. This gives children enough time to get into a project, experiment, and have discussion. In the typical public school, children often don't have sufficient time to delve into something before it's time to go on to something else. In some cases a workshop course is extended to one and a half hours, and for good reason. One such course is chess. The extra time is needed for children to learn theory, test theory, and play. Another extended course in a recent workshop was the one on film-making. This was done to give children enough time to assemble materials, set up what they were going to photograph, and do the filming. It's a process that can't be done well in less time.

We suggest that your organization consider one hour the minimum time for a course and extend the time according to the requirements proposed by the teacher. The teacher is the best judge of the time needed for children to get the most out of the course. We suggest that a single course not exceed two hours. For one thing, most parents prefer that their children take two one-hour courses for the money. Of course, in special programs—like the Society's hospital course—the whole morning might be spent in one place. Even so, children are not engaged in one single activity for more than an hour at a time.

Setting Tuition

Currently, the Gifted Child Society charges thirty dollars for a one-hour course and forty dollars for a one-and-a-half-hour course. Tuition is based on several factors: teachers' and administrators' salaries, rental of the building, custodial fees, cost of materials and equipment, and overhead expenses such as the cost of telephones and printing brochures and forms. Tuition also is affected by the size of classes. Our class average is between ten and sixteen students. If the student-teacher ratio is reduced further, then more teachers will have to be hired to teach fewer children. This raises the cost of tuition for each child.

Some courses charge a laboratory fee. This usually amounts to no more than five dollars. It pays for special materials or equipment used in that course. Parents pay five dollars extra for their child to be enrolled in "Model Rocketry" because each child is supplied with materials for constructing his or her own rocket.

The Society gives discounts for additional courses taken by a child and when more than one child from a family is enrolled. Each additional course is two dollars less than the tuition for the first course, down to a limit of twenty-four dollars. A child who takes three courses pays thirty dollars for the first course, twenty-eight dollars for the second, and twenty-six dollars for the third. If there are two children from the same family each taking one course, one child is assessed thirty dollars but the other pays only twenty-eight dollars.

All tuition charges and lab fees are payable at the time of registration.

Evaluating Student Performance

Parents should be able to arrange meetings with teachers at convenient times, usually before or after teachers' classes. Parents with questions about their children's progress should always have someone accessible to them. The school coordinator and some members of the school or curriculum committees should be on hand to speak with parents while classes are in session.

But the teacher should conduct some more formal evaluation of each child's performance and report it to the parents. The Gifted

Figure 13

THE SATURDAY WORKSHOPS

Sponsored by the Gifted Child Society, Inc.

Date:..

Dear Parent:

We are pleased to present our comments on your child in the classes
of the current Saturday Workshop semester.

STUDENT:.. Course..............................

Participation in Class:

Social Adjustment:

Growth:

Interest in Subject Area:

INSTRUCTOR'S REMARKS:

....
INSTRUCTOR'S SIGNATURE

Child Society supplies each teacher with evaluation forms for each child in his or her classes. The teachers also receive stamped, addressed envelopes to make it easier to mail forms home to parents. A child is evaluated at the conclusion of each course.

The Society does not use number or letter grades but relies instead on teacher observations and comments. These are recorded on the evaluation form (see fig. 13). Teachers are encouraged to make recommendations for continued intellectual growth and stimulation and to note difficulties that parents might help their children overcome.

A teacher makes a duplicate of every evaluation report for the child's file. On the duplicate form the teacher might note additional information that would be of interest to the school coordinator or other teachers. The teacher might say that a child needs to be with children of the same sex, that he has trouble working alone, that he lacks maturity, that she should not be in the same class with her brother, that he needs opportunities to exercise leadership, and the like.

The Society has a very liberal withdrawal policy. If a child is not enjoying a course for any reason, he can withdraw at any time with honor and a refund. If a child would rather be on the Little League field than in class, the Society makes every effort to put a bat in his hand instead of a pencil. If we were to suggest a motto that your organization could hang up wherever you operate your educational program, it might be this: "In all things, the children come first."

Chapter 14

Publicizing What You're Doing

There are many ways to publicize and advertise your organization and its educational program: newspaper articles, newspaper ads, radio announcements and talk shows, posters, leaflets, newsletters, personal letters to educators and other interested people, and public meetings you sponsor or send speakers to. Don't forget cable TV if there is a station operating in your area. What you do to publicize and advertise your organization and its activities, and when you do it, depends on what you want to accomplish.

Your organization should consider the following questions before deciding what kinds of publicity and advertising it will undertake:

• Do you want to begin slowly? Throughout the book we have cautioned against beginning too ambitiously. It's better to make small mistakes than whoppers. It's better to learn what to do when you still have time to learn. If your organization does want to begin slowly, it doesn't want to engage in a heavyweight publicity and advertising campaign.

• Do you want to reach a lot of people in a large area? If the answer is yes, then you will want to place publicity and advertising in large daily newspapers and on radio stations serving the area. If the answer is no, then you may want to limit publicity and advertising to one or two weekly newspapers and perhaps posters in public places, such as the public library.

• Do you want to reach a very select group? Suppose your organization wants to cater only to families in one town or in a neighborhood of a large city. In that case you might want to avoid newspaper and radio publicity and advertising altogether. It may be sufficient for your needs to place some posters in public places (library, banks, stores) and to mail a promotional letter or brochure to certain organizations and school officials.

• Will your organization's initial thrust be to create an educational program? Or does it wish to make parents of gifted children and the general public aware of the needs of gifted children and suggest ways to meet those needs? If the organization wants to begin by mounting just an information program, then the publicity might be primarily in the form of newspaper and radio news reports of what knowledgeable people have said about gifted children.

What's Newsworthy About What You're Doing?

In case you haven't noticed, education is big news. It's biggest in weekly newspapers and suburban daily newspapers. But news of education holds its own even in large city daily newspapers, on radio and television, and in magazines. Why? For two reasons. First, many people reading newspapers, listening to radio and watching TV are parents of school-age children. Second, many of the others who are reading, listening, and watching are paying high property taxes to support public education.

Because you're starting an organization for gifted children you are particularly newsworthy for these reasons:

1. Any organization has a good chance to get a response from local news media during its infancy. It probably can get space and time for a couple of announcements about the group forming, who's forming it, who's eligible to join, the purposes of the organization, where and when meetings are held, and where interested people can obtain additional information. Other news releases can report on meetings where officers are elected, by-laws are adopted, speakers are heard, and other business is decided.

2. Meeting the special needs of gifted children is still novel and controversial in many places. There continues to be considerable publicity about programs for handicapped children, but the quantity is not as great as it was in the sixties when attention was first being focused on the needs of the handicapped. Now, on every front—nationally, statewide, and locally—attention is increasingly being

directed to the needs of bright children and plans to meet those needs. There are people who think programs for gifted children are un-democratic because they create intellectual and social snobs, but there also used to be strong public reaction against doing anything for the mentally and physically handicapped. If you face hostile public opinion, use it to your advantage. The news media will be interested in a group that's attempting to organize in behalf of gifted children when that doesn't seem to be a popular thing to do. Underdogs and newcomers have friends in the press.

3. Your organization has appeal because it is non-profit, because it is being financed out of members' pockets, because it is for children, and because most of the work is done voluntarily by mothers and fathers who want to help their own children and the children of others.

4. If you operate an educational program, the nature of the program is newsworthy. The news media are generally interested in feature stories about people doing more than is expected of them. Undoubtedly your program will have many examples: a seven-year-old building and flying his own rocket, an eight-year-old demonstrating how to program a computer, a nine-year-old writing her own play.

Getting in Newspapers and on Radio

If you think newspapers are only interested in the sensational and print only what "sells newspapers," then you're wrong and might just as well forget about publicizing your organization. Perhaps the single biggest reason why some groups fail to get exposure is because they start off with a chip on their shoulder and somehow decide that either the media must accept news of their group on their terms or be damned. Unfortunately, it is usually the group that is damned. It is a classic example of biting off your nose to spite your face. Your organization needs the news media far more than they need you.

Here are some tips that can help you get the news media working for you by working with them:

1. Have your publicity chairperson visit or call newspaper editors or reporters and radio news or public service departments. Get to know who the organization will be dealing with and let them get to know your contact.

2. Find out the deadline for submitting news copy. Deadlines vary from newspaper to newspaper, and from radio station to radio station. Often a daily newspaper will have one deadline for suburban or organizational news, another for sports news and the comics page, and still another for page one. Know what the deadlines are and adhere to them.

3. Make sure your publicity chairperson knows how to get news to the proper person or place before the deadline. Some newspapers want all copy mailed or dropped off at the newspaper office; other newspapers encourage "drops" at such places as a police station or the news room of the municipal building; still others prefer that news—particularly of night meetings—be called in to a reporter or stenographer.

4. Find out what the policies are for accepting photographs and other illustrations. Some newspapers prefer to send their own photographers. Your publicity chairperson will have to know how to arrange for a photographer to be assigned and what kind of picture to set up for him. Other newspapers, particularly weekly newspapers, want photographs submitted with the copy. Most newspapers insist on black and white glossy prints.

5. Ask the people at the newspapers and radio stations what kinds of news they are looking for. Some will want everything your organization can supply. Others will say they're looking primarily for feature stories on what children are doing and will take an occasional news article on a special, outstanding speaker; but they don't want reports of routine business meetings.

How to Write a News Release

We can't give your publicity chairperson a quickie journalism course, but we do want to give him or her enough tips on news writing to help your group succeed in publicizing its activities.

1. We have consistently used the word "publicity" when speaking about the material you will be submitting to the news media. What you send in will be judged on the basis of its newsworthiness. Consequently, you may think it's a good idea to let everyone know the names of all your commitee chairpersons and commitee members, but the news media may cut out the lists for fear of putting their readers or listeners to sleep. Try to keep in mind that your news

releases should be just that—releases of news. Forget the strictly inside stuff that most people won't be interested in anyway. And don't editorialize or engage in backslapping: "Everyone thought the program was terrific." "The refreshments were delicious." "All students thoroughly enjoyed the fine presentation." Just the straight facts!

2. In writing an article about a meeting of your organization or when announcing your educational program, lead off with the most important news. If the most important thing at a membership meeting was the address by a local superintendent of schools, start off with his remarks. Don't write a news story like the minutes of the meeting. You want to maintain the interest of the reader or listener for as long as posible. And if the newspaper or radio station has to shorten your copy, it will work from the end forward—cutting the least important first.

3. Keep sentences and paragraphs short. This is especially true for radio copy. Remember that radio copy must be listened to. A radio audience will not be able to handle long, rambling sentences. Until the publicity chairperson gets the knack of writing copy, he or she should go over the copy estimating the average number of words per sentence and the number of words with more than three syllables. The average number of words should be around 17. Seventy percent of the words in Lincoln's Gettysburg Address contain five letters or less. Your copy should do as well.

4. End a page with the end of a paragraph and begin the next page with a new paragraph. This is particularly important for newspapers, where copy is still set in hot lead on a linotype machine. One page of copy is handed to one linotypist and another page to another linotypist. The man setting page 2 can't go hunting for page 3 to see where the last sentence goes. Writing copy this way can also help prevent errors when a typist goes quickly from page to page.

5. Double and triple check all names, dates, figures, times, and other facts. If your publicity chairperson is writing about the educational program, he or she should be sure that the right times go with the right courses, that the address and phone number of the school coordinator are correct, and that teachers' names are complete and accurate. Your organization could be in for some real headaches if the tuition is listed at twenty dollars instead of thirty dollars, or if people who want brochures are supposed to call 476-5532 and the copy reads 476-5523.

6. Don't leave out important details. Something is obviously missing from this sentence: "Reginald Petrie, curriculum coordinator of the Association for Bright Children, announced the addition of five new courses to the Saturday morning workshop." The names of the courses were left out. If the writer doesn't know what the courses are, then it's better to leave Mr. Petrie's statement out altogether.

7. Give information that will make the article lively and interesting to read. If your publicity chairperson or someone else is writing an article about the hospital seminar like the one conducted by the Gifted Child Society, prime ingredients would be quotations from ᵆpital staff members and children. Compare these two paragraphs:

a. One of the places visited by the children was the operating room. It is normally closed to visitors. Miss Rosemary James, chief operating room nurse, explained how the room is used and the children asked questions and examined the equipment.

b. "This is the first time anyone other than doctors, nurses, and patients has been admitted to the operating room," said Miss Rosemary James, chief operating room nurse. She showed children the operating room equipment and explained how it works. The children fired a barrage of questions at Miss James. "Can a heart be transplanted here?" asked one child. "No," Miss James replied, "we don't have the right equipment." Another child wondered if there is more than one kind of anesthetic. "There are at least three kinds used in the operating room," Miss James said.

8. Rewrite. Before turning copy in, go over it once or twice to make sure the article says what it is supposed to say and can easily be understood. News copy must communicate accurately and quickly.

9. Type and double-space copy on standard typing paper, 8½ by 11 inches. Start the first page of the article about half way down the page so the editor can use of the top of the page for a headline. At the bottom of all pages except the final one, write the word "more." At the end of the article, write "30" or the number sign, #.

10. Type a couple of key words at the top of page one to indicate the nature of the article. The article on the in-hospital program might be tagged "Children Tour Hospital." On succeeding pages of the article, write at the top: "Add 1—Children Tour," "Add 2—Children Tour," and so on. "Add 1" would be the equivalent of page two.

11. Be sure the article states at the top of page one where it originates, the date of release, and the name of someone the newspaper or radio station can contact for more information. For example:

From: The Association for Bright Children
P.O. Box 100, Bigtown
For Release: March 28, 1975
Contact: Mrs. Ruth Hubbard (736-4819)

A Word About Advertising

The Gifted Child Society has used ads in local newspapers with good results. An early ad contained only copy. More recent ones have included a photo. Both kinds of ads have drawn well. It is suggested that if your organization advertises its educational program and uses a photo, the picture should show one or two children engaged in an activity.

Your organization may have one or two members in the advertising profession who are willing to offer suggestions, write copy, and draft layouts. If not, you can always get help from the advertising department of the newspapers and radio stations you plan to use for your advertising.

The important thing to remember about a newspaper ad is that it has to have immediate visual impact and holding value. In one Society ad the top half showed a child sculpting. The copy began by listing some of the courses offered by the workshop. The first course listed was "Six-Legged Science," a guaranteed eye-catcher. An ad for a summer session began: "This Summer . . . Challenge Your Gifted Child."

Of course, the ad must tell readers when the educational program is given, where it is given, what children are eligible, and where to write or call for more information. Don't try to squeeze in everything. It not only gets expensive that way, but you also will give readers more than they want in a single dose.

When working with a newspaper advertising department, you do not have to supply the ad in its final form. You don't even have to design the ad for large papers. However, we do suggest that you supply, in addition to the copy and photograph, a rough layout showing where the copy and photograph are supposed to go. Your layout should either be the exact size of the ad or a version drawn to scale.

Use a box to show where you want your picture. If the first line of your ad says, "At Last, Help for Bright Children," show on your layout where that line should go. The newspaper will set the line in an appropriate size type.

The ad doesn't have to be big to be effective. Ads run by the Society have never exceeded two columns in width or six inches in depth. Ads used in the early days of the organization were much smaller. Also, the cost of an ad can vary with the size of the newspaper. An ad in a daily newspaper with a large circulation will cost far more than an ad in a small weekly newspaper. Your group, therefore, might want to place a two-column by six-inch ad in the weekly newspaper and a one-column by four-inch ad in the daily newspaper. You will have to pay more for ads in color and for placement of ads on particular pages. We suggest, therefore, that your ads be black and white and that they be placed run-of-paper (ROP). That is, the newspaper chooses where they will go.

Every newspaper and radio station can supply you with rate cards showing the cost for different size ads. The card also lists deadlines for copy.

An example of a recent ad for the Gifted Child Society is in Appendix E.

Publishing a Newsletter

Eventually your organization will want to publish a newsletter for circulation among members and friends. The newsletter should contain articles about the organization and its educational program and also articles about what's happening for or with gifted children outside your organization. If the Congress or the state legislature is debating a bill on education for the gifted, your newsletter should have a report. It is also desirable to use the columns of the newsletter to help parents in your organization. For example, each issue might contain a single question-and-answer feature. Questions such as: "If my child says he's bored in school, what should I do?" "How do I get my son interested in something besides science?" or "My daughter wants to advance in sculpting; do you have any suggestions?" might be answered by people within the organization or outside experts. Outside experts might include a researcher at a nearby college, a teacher, a school administrator, or a psychologist.

Other desirable newsletter features are reports on the educational program of your group, a summary of the activities of the executive board, and some contributions from the children in the form of poems, student council reports, etc.

In the Gifted Child Society, the person who writes articles for the news media is not the same person who is in charge of the newsletter. The two jobs would be burdensome, even for someone with experience in one or both jobs. It is useful if the newsletters' editor has some experience in writing and with graphics. The editor may ask of the organization and others to write articles or parts of articles. However, it should be the editor's responsibility to rewrite any or all copy according to the style and specifications established for the newsletter. Also, he or she should not be afraid to ask someone who submitted copy to rewrite it if it's in bad shape.

Because editors come and go, there should be a set policy for the newsletter. It should be established which features are a regular part of the newsletter and which are up to the discretion of the editor. The policy also should establish any reasonable taboos. For example, a prohibition against endorsements of commercial educational materials or games.

In laying out the pages of the newsletter (positioning articles and illustrations), the editor does not have to be fancy, but he or she may welcome some advice:

• Use headlines that are larger in size than the body type. If you send out your copy to be processed by a printer, this is no problem. If you are typing a mimeograph stencil, try using a primary typewriter (large letter size) or an IBM Selectric typewriter for headlines. The IBM machine has interchangeable type balls and you can get a larger size for your headlines.

• Headlines not only attract readers to articles, they serve to break up the columns of body type. If the newsletter has long articles, it is always a good idea to put in a small headline every two or three paragraphs. If a printer is preparing your newsletter, these headlines can be the same size as the body type but darker, bold face. If you are doing the work yourself, you might use the same size type as the body but make the small headlines all capital letters. Be sure to leave at least one line of space above and below the small headlines.

• Another effective layout device is to box in small, important articles and announcements with rules. This calls attention to the item and the box also breaks up columns of body type.

• Every inch of every column and page does not have to be crowded with type. A little white space between articles opens up a page and makes it easier for the reader.

• If you are mimeographing your newsletter and cannot use photographs, or if you want to cut down on the use of photographs to save money, there are other ways to illustrate. Drawings, charts and graphs can be effective illustrations. If you are preparing copy for offset reproduction, you can purchase whole sheets of stock illustrations from an artist supply store or good stationer's.

• A column should not be more than about three inches wide. If articles run the full width of a page, it becomes taxing for the reader. Actually, column widths can vary; have some articles run in columns about two inches wide and some three inches wide.

Check with your local postmaster for information regarding the mailing of newsletters. Your organization probably qualifies as a non-profit organization. This allows you to mail third class for a cheaper rate.

This is a good place to remind you that your organization should keep a scrapbook and keep it up-to-date. The scrapbook should include newspaper clippings about the organization's activities, and perhaps about education for the gifted in general, copies of newsletters, brochures, and announcements about your educational program, advertising copy and ads as they appeared, and anything else considered important and not kept elsewhere.

Chapter 15

Winning Friends and Influencing People

We think that the cause for gifted children is now on the threshold of acceptance. The federal government and many state governments are beginning to provide encouragement, funds, and expert help to improve the educational opportunities for bright children. As the U.S. Commissioner of Education pointed out in 1971, gifted children are in a very real sense handicapped. When they are turned off by education and are thwarted in their attempts to realize their potential, they are indeed deprived. And so, to a great extent, is the society that allows it to happen. Your organization, as it grows in experience and stature, will want to take its place with the Gifted Child Society and other independent agencies in an effort to increase support for publicly financed programs for gifted and talented children.

Helping Gifted Children Is a National Cause

During the summer of 1973, the Senate Subcommittee on Education conducted public hearings on a proposed Gifted and Talented Education Assistance Act. The executive director of the Gifted Child Society was one of those who testified before the committee. Part of her testimony consisted of reading letters from children in the Society who expressed in their own words why they needed help. The executive director also submitted her written testimony (Appendix F), which comments on the various provisions of the legislation.

We have already pointed out that in 1970 officials of the Gifted Child Society testified before the federal regional commissioner in preparation for his report on gifted and talented children. It was the U.S. Commissioner's report to the Congress that caused it to draft legislation such as the Gifted and Talented Education Assistance Act.

Here's how your organization can help in the national effort.

• Contact your senators and representatives in Congress and tell them of your concern for public support of public programs for the gifted and talented. Ask them for their views on such support and, specifically, on pending legislation. To those representatives and senators who are unsympathetic to the needs of gifted children, offer your organization's help in gathering information, providing written or oral testimony, or or assisting in any other way they might see fit. To those who are unsympathetic, provide them with information and views out of your organization and from other sources in order to help acquaint them with the need.

• Remain alert. Keep track of legislation before the Congress and testimony before committees.

• Write the U.S. Office of Education of the Gifted and Talented in Washington and let officials there know of the existence of your organization. Explain what you are doing. Ask if there is anything your group can do to help the office in its efforts to work with state and local agencies on behalf of gifted and talented children. Write either Harold C. Lyon, Jr., Director, or Mrs. Jane Case Williams, Deputy Director. The address is

> U.S. Office of Education of the Gifted and Talented
> Room 2100, ROB 3
> HEW,
> Washington, D.C. 20202.

Where Can You Get More Information?

Your organization would do well to start its own library of books, pamphlets, articles, and speeches on the gifted and talented. But your library and/or research committee should monitor newspapers and magazines for articles pertaining to bright children.

In Chapter 4 we referred you to the ERIC Information Clearinghouse for Handicapped and Gifted, Reston, Virginia. Your organization should get on its mailing list.

Also, contact the office of your state education department that deals with education for the gifted. Ask to be put on a mailing list for any information issued by them. That office also might inform you of other organizations in your state and region so that an exchange of newsletters, brochures, and views can be arranged.

Subscribe to state education journals issued by the education department, teachers' organization, school board association, and other agencies. These publications often contain articles of interest, and they can also alert your group to upcoming meetings or seminars on the gifted to which you might want to send representatives.

Lobbying for State and Federal Legislation

As a non-profit organization you are prevented by federal law from spending "substantial" time and money on lobbying. And you are forbidden to actively campaign for political candidates. But the law does not prevent your organization from spending *some* time on lobbying.

The lobbying should be low key. You can write your representatives in Congress, for example. Your organization also should be in touch with state representatives, particularly those legislators who appear to be most interested in passing legislation on behalf of gifted children and those who are members of the education committee. Much of the legislation passed on behalf of mentally and physically handicapped children was prompted by steady pressure from organizations of parents of handicapped children. There is no reason why parents of gifted children should not exert the same kind of pressure.

"Pressure" includes letting legislators know as often as possible that your organization represents people who care, and vote, and that you are concerned about the federal and state governments' meeting the needs of gifted children. Be sure to thank your legislators when they evidence support in letters to you, in speeches on the floor of Congress or in the state legislature, and in voting for worthwhile laws. Good lobbying is not badgering, it is providing information that really can be of help to a legislator. Let him know that you are aware of bills being considered or reports being filed. Urge him to support worthwhile legislation, and to draft legislation, and congratulate him when he does.

The following are two excerpts from letters sent by the Society's executive director to Senator Harrison Williams of New Jersey:

I am writing in behalf of our over 2,000 active and current members to express our pleasure and appreciation in connection with the introduction of an updated version of last year's bill for educational assistance for gifted and talented children. You may be sure that our entire membership is grateful for your interest in an area which is very close to our hearts.

I am writing in behalf of all our members to urge you to restore the term "education of gifted and talented" as an area of responsibility under the new titles of the Elementary and Secondary Education Act's Support Services and Innovation. We are glad to know that you are a friend of the gifted.

Another way your organization might be effective is to invite local legislators to your meetings. You might also ask a state or federal legislator to address your membership at a public meeting which your organization widely publicizes. The legislator will know your strength as well as your interest. It's a good way to begin a relationship between your group and your representatives in government. You also may want to consider inviting them to visit your educational program in session.

As you begin your organization and its educational program, you may be too busy to do much of what we have been suggesting. But it would be well if your group could make the effort at the first opportunity.

Going from Here to There

What to Do and When to Do It

At the Start

A few parents of gifted children and possibly some interested educators meet informally.

At Six Months

When at least fifty parents of gifted children and interested educators are ready, a formal organization is created. The group establishes goals, writes a constitution and by-laws, and elects officers and trustees. Activities are publicized.

First Year

An educational program of no more than two classes, or thirty-five students, is begun; children seven to ten are enrolled.

At One and a Half Years

The eduational program is expanded to include no more than seventy students. Age groups are expanded, but no more than one age or grade level is added in any one semester.

Second Year

The educational program is expanded to 100 students, assuming that it is operating smoothly. A school coordinator is hired as a part-time employee. Based on experience to date, educational goals are determined, and policies regarding curriculum, staff, and class size are decided. A newsletter to be circulated among members is begun.

At Two and a Half Years

The educational program is expanded by no more than twenty-five percent.

Third through Fifth Year

The enrollment, number of classes, and size of faculty are increased by no more than ten percent during any one semester. Constitution and by-laws are reviewed in light of experience. A scholarship program is begun on a small scale.

Fifth Year

The educational program is growing, but limits on the enrollment and size of the operation are adopted to maintain quality control. The hiring of a part-time curriculum coordinator is considered if the number of courses is almost twenty.

Sixth Year

Community involvement and legislative action committees are at work assisting local school districts to start their own programs for gifted and talented children and pressing for legislation to benefit all gifted and talented children. The organization is participating in conferences and providing speakers for other groups.

Seventh Year and Beyond

When the membership reaches 500 or more, an executive secretary is hired. The organization is actively assisting school districts as they initiate their own programs for gifted and talented children. The group is contributing its ideas, based on experience, to state and national agencies concerned with helping the gifted and talented.

Conclusion

In this book the Gifted Child Society of New Jersey has tried to be a guide and a friend to other parents of gifted children. In sharing our experiences and accumulated knowledge with you, we have intended to help you as you and your friends and neighbors start out.

We have reviewed all that we have said and have distilled the essential elements to these key points:

1. Don't try to do too much too soon. Sometimes it is hard even for the Gifted Child Society to look back and remember how it all began with a handful of concerned mothers. But we do reflect, and we always conclude that had we been overambitious, the whole effort might have gotten out of control and foundered. We're glad we started small and had big thoughts. We recommend you do likewise.

2. The children come first in everything. That sounds like a throwaway line, but it isn't. We're sure you have attended enough school meetings to know that the concern for children's welfare is not always uppermost. Don't let your organization become something to satisfy adults—socially or politically. Make sure it remains focused on helping gifted children.

3. Set real, honest and attainable goals for your organization. The group that has nothing worthwhile to strive for probably won't strive for anything. We suggest that the goals encompass your determination to serve gifted children in your organization, their parents, and the greater cause of gifted children around the country. The goals you agree up on should be set down in your constitution and by-laws and followed in actual practice. If the membership no longer believes in a goal, change it, but don't set a direction and then go another way.

4. We think that the most important thing your organization can do for your gifted children is to conduct an out-of-school enrichment program and at the same time create a public awareness of their special needs. After many, and sometimes heated, debates, the Gifted Child Society still believes that gifted children need to associate with other gifted children who may share their ability and interests.

5. The educational program provided by your organization should enrich gifted children's experiences in the sciences, humanities, and the arts and unlock their leadership potential.

6. As you build your own organization and serve your own children and parents, please remember that there is a larger cause. The federal government and many states have started to do important things on behalf of gifted children. Active, well-informed parents like those in your organization are necessary to make sure that the effort continues.

We leave you with these thoughts. We hope they serve you well, and we wish you success and luck.

Part II
FOR TEACHERS OF GIFTED CHILDREN

Chapter 16

Characteristics of the Gifted Child

Gifted children are children who do things a little earlier, a little better, a little faster, and probably a little differently than most other children.

Potential and Abilities

Some gifted children are capable at a very early age of dealing with abstract concepts, working on more than one level simultaneously, or coping with more than one idea at a time. Indeed, they seem to thrive on this kind of multiple exposure.

A teacher of the Gifted Child Society says he continues to be amazed by the way children in his class are able to start with a fairly simple idea and proceed quickly to explore it from ever more complex angles. Gifted children like to create, invent, investigate, conceptualize, and exercise leadership ability. And they are very good at it.

Self-motivation

Not every gifted child is motivated. Unfortunately, in some cases a child's natural motivation and insatiable curiosity may have been blunted by bad experiences in school. However, you will discover that most gifted children can learn independently if given necessary guidance and direction by you, and if they are in the kind of learning climate that encourages individual study and experimentation.

Stick-to-itiveness

In a typical public school classroom there will be a goodly number of children who will probe, question, or study only as long or as far as they are required to. The gifted child is capable of a longer attention span than would be expected for someone of his age. And it is not unusual for a gifted child to pursue an interest on his own until he has exhausted all the research possibilities available to him.

The Need to Be an Active Learner

Gifted children are seldom passive learners. One of the Society's teachers has said that a child in the typical classroom is expected to receive information and respond to the questions and directions of the teacher. But the gifted child wants always to be involved, to be doing, to be asking questions, to be applying what he has learned. He is restless, both intellectually and physically.

Leadership

One of the reasons for the current national concern about the learning opportunities available to gifted children is the fear that the nation may ignore many of its potential leaders if it ignores the needs of gifted children. The gifted child has leadership capabilities because of several other factors: (1) he knows his own mind and his own abilities better than most people know theirs; (2) he has a keener insight into the thinking, abilities, and motivations of others; (3) he has an unusual capacity to look at problems and their alternative solutions from many angles and to reason out the proper course to follow, and (4) he has a highly developed sense of social and moral responsibility.

Emotional Development

Most gifted children are very verbal; they talk a lot, and tend to be very active people. They may become angered or depressed when frustrated in their attempts to go in directions they want to and are capable of going. Above all, gifted children behave as children. We point out later, when discussing discipline, the importance of keeping in mind that a seven-year-old gifted child is a seven-year-old child. He may think like someone older, but he is only seven.

Chapter 17

Establishing Goals for You and Your Students

In the latter half of the sixties, the Institute of Administrative Research at Teachers College, Columbia University, began work on a project called Indicators of Quality (IOQ). The purposes of the project were (1) to determine what constituted quality in the teaching/learning process, (2) what activities in the classroom most encouraged quality, and (3) how often and how well those activities were conducted in America's public schools.

Groups of educators and nearly 40,000 laymen were asked to identify what they thought was most indicative of quality in the teaching/learning process. Their observations boiled down to four essential ingredients of quality education:

1. *Individualization.* Individual differences among children are recognized, appreciated, and catered to.

2. *Interpersonal Regard.* Children demonstrate trust and respect for each other and for the teacher (notwithstanding occasional and natural clashes), and the teacher demonstrates trust and respect for the children.

3. *Creativity.* The teacher recognizes that ability can be expressed in different ways, and therefore encourages varied use of talents and intellectual experimentation.

4. *Group Activity.* Interaction between teacher and students and between students and students aids learning for most children and encourages their social development.

The Institute of Administrative Research went into more than 20,000 classrooms to find out what activities were most apt to encourage individualization, interpersonal regard, creativity, and group activity. According to chief researcher Dr. Martin N. Olson, the Indicators of Quality were most apparent where there was a high incidence of "small group work, individual work, discussion, laboratory work, pupil report, and demonstration." The Indicators of Quality were most likely not to be present where there was a high incidence of teacher lecture and "seat work." Unfortunately for American school children, the Institute's researchers discovered more lecturing and seat work going on than the other activities.

What's the Purpose of Teaching and Learning?

While the Institute is concerned with all classrooms in all public schools, we are concerned here with classrooms for gifted children. What the Institute found desirable for all classrooms is most essential in classrooms for gifted children. The teacher of gifted children, then, might look to the work of the Institute as he drafts overall goals for himself and his students. These broad goals might be stated as follows:

1. In order to create a climate in which gifted children can flourish and the teacher can function at his best, children should be encouraged to strive for their individual learning goals and to fulfill their individual needs for expression.

2. Children should be encouraged to respect each other's views and needs and the teacher's role as learning facilitator. The teacher should respect the unique abilities of children and their need to exercise those abilities in different ways.

3. Children should be encouraged to learn in a variety of ways, including, but not necessarily limited to, the following: individual study, experimentation, and expression; lively group discussion and debate; and research and project development involving small groups.

In addition to establishing broad goals for the classroom, you will want to determine specific learning goals and lesson objectives for the course or courses you are teaching. A number of examples of the kinds of goals and objectives we are talking about can be seen in the lesson plans shown and discussed later. The following overall learning goal and lesson objectives are from a course about the customs, dress, heritage, and living conditions of people in other countries.

Overall learning goal: To learn how other children in other parts of the world differ from American children, while recognizing how they are similar in their basic needs, beliefs and behavior.

Lesson objectives: (1) To know what basic needs children share; (2) to know how to locate places on a map (study Mexico); (3) to know how to follow map directions and find proper routes (study Amish people in U.S.); (4) to practice map use and following directions (study Japan); and (5) to know how large Africa is and how diverse are its people.

All Gifted Children Don't Learn Alike

In every classroom in every public school there is a wide range of intellectual abilities, needs, and limitations for learning. In every classroom for gifted children there is a similar range, though somewhat narrower. The teacher of gifted children should not assume that because all of the children in the room have been labeled gifted they will all be able to learn the same thing in the same way at the same time. Among any group of gifted children, some will be more gifted than others, some will be more motivated than others, some will be more mature than others, some will want to do more for themselves than others, some will be more reticent than others, some will learn faster than others, and so it goes. Remember the goal that encourages individuals to be individuals, and remember to respect individual differences.

There are many ways to learn, and you should encourage children to attempt as many as suit their abilities and needs. The following catalog of seven learning activities might be helpful.

Individual research and experimentation. It is not unusual in elementary schools to find only teachers conducting experiments while students look on. It is not unusual in many schools to find different children engaged in the same kind of research at the same time. Many gifted children of elementary school age, however, are both anxious and able to conduct their own experiments, under proper guidance. While you will want children to learn certain lessons from their experiments, you should allow and encourage children to approach the end result in somewhat different ways. One child might use similar materials and techniques as others to arrive at the proper conclusion but use them differently from the child working next to him. Provide some opportunity for children to make up their own open-ended experiments and arrive at their own conclusions and findings. With proper direction, most gifted children are able to undertake research on an individual basis.

Again, not all gifted children are ready at the same time to take on the same amount of individual work.

Individual reading and writing. One of the Gifted Child Society teachers said that when he first taught five and six-year-olds, he had to keep reminding himself that the children already could read. Most of the children were reading at a second- or third-grade level. You can expect, then, that gifted children probably will learn faster from reading than other children. Also, most gifted children will benefit by reading at their own pace. Many gifted children have an exceptional ability for self-expression. Those that don't obviously should not be forced into situations that will embarrass or frighten them. For those capable of self-expression, provide opportunities for writing in styles and on subjects that allow them the freedom they need.

Discussion, debate and problem solving. Since gifted children tend to be more inquisitive and more verbal than other children, they generally learn much and quickly through the lively exchange of ideas and opinions. Many teachers have described the speed by which gifted children, through free and spirited discussion, move from a fairly simple idea to more complex and varied concepts. Through debate, gifted children often are able to examine an idea from many angles and come away with a variety of interpretations.

Role playing. Because gifted children tend to be more adept at self-expression, there should be opportunities, particularly in the language arts and the performing arts, for them to act the parts of characters in music, drama, literature, and history. Some teachers at the Gifted Child Society have found children successfully turned on by the chance to role play animals and inanimate objects. Imagine the challenge to a child's gift for self-expression and inventiveness if he is able to act the part of a giraffe or of a redwood tree growing up through the centuries.

Group work: Probably no gifted child desires, or should be encouraged, to work alone most of the time. While many gifted children are more capable of working successfully on an individual basis, they do need the companionship, competition and the stimulation of other gifted children. Discussion and role playing are group activities, but there also should be opportunities for children to learn by doing experiments, research, and projects in groups of varying sizes. As with individual work, know what basic skills you want groups of children to learn under your direction. But give them the freedom to go in slightly different directions and to go beyond what is expected of them.

Field trip. Children can learn by going outside the classroom to see things, do things, and ask questions of other people. It is necessary with gifted children to make more of the field trip experience than may be true for other children. If a group of gifted children visits a computer center, it is likely they will want to see more and ask more questions than other children would. That may mean that in addition to a guide you will want to make sure that there is a programmer, technician, and perhaps even an engineer standing by. You may want to advise your hosts that they should be prepared to show and demonstrate more computer processes and, if possible, allow children to try their hand at certain activities.

Lecture. While this activity goes on much of the time in the typical school classroom, it should be the least important activity in the class for gifted children. We don't mean to imply that gifted children have nothing to learn from a lecture by their teacher or other resource persons. They do. But lectures should be used sparingly as learning activities. We mentioned other resource persons. A program for gifted children, particularly when conducted out of school, has a special freedom to bring into the classroom whomever the teacher wants. It is the wise teacher who takes advantage of this opportunity. Be sure to suggest to speakers to lecture with aids whenever possible. These might include slides, films, photos, objects, demonstrations, animals, artifacts, and the like. Lecturers should be short on presentation and long on answers to far-ranging and probing questions.

Basic Skills. Because gifted children are usually such rapid learners, teachers will need to keep a constant check that no basic skills are overlooked.

Chapter 18

Preparing to Teach

The Gifted Child Society requires no syllabus. It does not dictate to teachers how they should teach, what the learning goals should be, or what materials they should use. Teachers do this themselves, and they do it with the help of lesson plans.

While the Society requires lesson plans from teachers to make sure they have considered the direction in which they and the children are heading, the real benefit of the lesson plans is to the teacher. By writing out a plan for each lesson, the teacher decides on the basic information or concepts he or she will teach and what materials and equipment he or she will need. Lesson plans encourage the teacher to organize learning so that fact builds upon fact, and the experience of weeks one and two make possible the experiences of weeks three and four.

Writing a Lesson Plan

The Society provides teachers with forms for their use in outlining lesson plans, but they are optional. There is no set pattern for the lesson plan. Some lesson plans imply learning goals by describing activities. Other lesson plans start off with objectives or goals clearly stated. Some teachers use still other ways to outline their lessons. On the following pages we show actual lesson plans written by Gifted Child Society teachers. The plans are in different subject areas and demonstrate a variety of styles in constructing lesson plans.

The first set of lesson plans is for a course called "The World of Tomorrow." Designed for children six and seven, the course intends for children to understand what future developments might affect their lives. The teacher has divided the ten lessons into different topics: cars, food, homes, clothes, etc. For each lesson, the teacher has planned a lead-off discussion, followed by a demontsration and an activity for children to engage in. You will notice that in each discussion period children start talking about things from the past and present before they are asked to imagine what might be in the future. These lesson plans are quite structured.

The second set of lesson plans also is quite structured. The plans are for a course called "Science for Beginners," offered to children five and six years old. In these plans, the teacher begins each outline with a statement of the learning goal in the form of a question. Demonstrations and experiments are briefly described and materials needed are listed.

The third course outline is for a course called "Politics and Economics for the Elementary School Child." This is an exceptionally detailed outline of what the teacher wants the children to accomplish and what will happen in class during the ten-week period. This set of lesson plans also is included because of the unusual nature of the course.

Gifted Child Society
Tentative Lesson Outline

Instructor:
Course: The World of Tomorrow
Age Group: 6 - 7 years
Hour: 11:00 - 12:00

Demonstration

- "Amaze-a-matic" — the car that can be programmed.
- SSP—no gas, no battery

  (gyroscope principal)

Outline for 1st week's lesson

"Cars"

Discuss:

- cars of the past (Pictures)
- today: problems, features that were "unbelievable" 50 yrs. ago
- future autos

Activity:

- hover cars of the future
- design own, enter the race!

Materials:

- Sheets of thin styrofoam
- String, balloons, tape, crayons, straws, scissors

Gifted Child Society
Tentative Lesson Outline

Instructor:
Course: The World of Tomorrow
Age Group: 6 - 7 years
Hour: 11:00 - 12:00

Demonstration:

- sampling of cooked seaweed, dried veg.'s
- teaching computer made by 3rd graders
- how electricity can be used

Materials:

- wire, bulbs, batteries, Fahnstock clamps, plastic cases, product pictures

Outline for 2nd week's lesson
                    "Food"

Discuss:

- problem of hunger today
- farmers of yesterday and today
- future ideas—watering desert, fish farms, ocean farms
- computerized shopping

Activity:

- computerized supermarket (each child will choose a product and program his computer to light when activated.) We'll go shopping!

Gifted Child Society
Tentative Lesson Outline

Instructor:
Course: The World of Tomorrow
Age Group: 6 - 7 years
Hour: 11:00 - 12:00

Demonstration:

- "Robot" pantomime game

Activity:

- shoebox diorama of a future room

Materials:

- shoeboxes, cardboard, crayons, markers, playdoh, material, carpet and tile pieces

Outline for 3rd week's lesson
"Homes"

Discuss:

- homes around the world (even animal homes).

- heating and lighting in the past

- houses of the future: self-cleaning, robots, cardboard houses, moveable walls, TV

Gifted Child Society
Tentative Lesson Outline

Instructor:

Course: The World of Tomorrow

Age Group: 6 - 7 years

Hour: 11:00 - 12:00

Activity:

- clothes of future advertisements (as on TV). (Each child designs and cuts from cloth, paper, or preferred media — "sell" item and its fantastic capabilities.)

Outline for 4th week's lesson
                              "Clothes"

Discuss:

- clothes of past; clothes of other countries, clothes today

- possibilities and dangers in clothing

Demonstration:

- Scotchguard experiments on staining.

Materials:

- Scotchguard, various materials, pictures, scissors.

Gifted Child Society
Tentative Lesson Outline

Instructor:
Course: The World of Tomorrow
Age Group: 6 - 7 years
Hour: 11:00 - 12:00

Activity:

- design mod shape on thin wood or similar medium, cut out with dremel saw. Sand, put hold with drill. Wear as desired.

Outline for 5th week's lesson
"Jewelry"

Discuss:

- jewelry of past and other countries (brooch, cameo, mosaic pins, Indian beads)
- Jewelry today and in the future

Demonstration:

- Various jewelry items to touch and try (mirror)

Materials:

- saw, drill, wood, leather laces, sandpaper

Gifted Child Society
Tentative Lesson Outline

Instructor:
Course: The World of Tomorrow
Age Group: 6 - 7 years
Hour: 11:00 - 12:00

Activity:

- 3 large frieze drawings of the 3 possibilities for cities in 2000

Materials:

- large papers, markers, paints

Outline for 6th week's lesson
"Cities Weather"

Discuss:

- weather folklore and suspicions (truisms too)
- today's weather satellite
- cities of the future and how they hope to plan the weather (underground cities, underwater floating cities, domed city).

Demonstration:

- flannel board illustration of the water cycle
- evaporation experiment

Gifted Child Society
Tentative Lesson Outline

Instructor:

Course: The World of Tomorrow

Age Group: 6 - 7 years

Hour: 11:00 - 12:00

Activity:

- make an art museum of the future. Use wide variety of media—paint, sponges, styrofoam, cloth, paper, sticks, etc. (Each child creates his own museum piece.)

Outline for 7th week's lesson

"Art"

Discuss:

- free time, hobbies, recreations, talents
- folk art, famous paintings and statues
- modern art; future possibilities

Demonstration:

- The creative color machine

Materials:

- as Activity, also markers, pencils, scissors, glue

Gifted Child Society
Tentative Lesson Outline

Instructor:
Course: The World of Tomorrow
Age Group: 6 - 7 years
Hour: 11:00 - 12:00

Activity:

- using the tape recorder for unusual effects—reversing music and speech of each child
- creative dance to short selection

Materials:

- as above
- postcards & related pictures

Outline for 8th week's lesson

"Music"

Discuss:

- music of the past and in other countries
- music today and in 2000

Demonstration:

- Mexican hat dance
- early phonograph (if possible)
- 78 rpm records
- recording of "The Planets"—futuristic

Gifted Child Society
Tentative Lesson Outline

Instructor:
Course: The World of Tomorrow
Age Group: 6 - 7 years
Hour: 11:00 - 12:00

Activity:

- Mock trip to another planet
  —purchase tickets
  —plan trip, pack, etc.
  —travel through space, land,
  —explore

Outline for 9th week's lessons

"Space"

Discuss:

- how early people felt about the stars and moon
- our moon landing and future possibilities

Demonstration:

- rocket take-off

Materials:

- pictures

Gifted Child Society
Tentative Lesson Outline

Instructor:

Course: The World of Tomorrow

Age Group: 6 - 7 years

Hour: 11:00 - 12:00

Activity:

- What's next? Each child will invent something new, draw, name and explain invention. Patents issued to each.

Discuss:

- inventions of the past (Franklin, Edison, Bell, Salk)
- modern way of life (money, jobs, recreation)
- jets, travel, modern conveniences

Demonstration:

- (pictures) tour of some recent inventions

Materials:

- drawing paper, markers, crayons, pictures

Outline for 10th week's lesson

"Inventions & Discoveries"

Gifted Child Society
Tentative Lesson Outline

Instructor:
Course: Science for Beginners
Hour: 11:00 A.M.   Age: 6-7

Outline for 1st week's lesson

How do scientists think and work?

  I. Problems that face children & their parents

    A. List situations that are puzzling

    B. Classify in various ways these problems

 II. Organize steps in good thinking

    A. Apply steps to familiar situations

    B. Apply steps to scientific situations

III. Sensitive scientific instruments

    A. Observations using instruments

    B. Observations without instruments

    C. Comparison & contrast differences

Materials: microprojector, microscopes, magnifying glasses, etc.

Gifted Child Society
Tentative Lesson Outline

Instructor:

Course: Science for Beginners

Hour: 11:00 A.M.   Age: 6-7

Outline for 2nd week's lesson

What are the main groups of living things?

I. Orientation to living things in immediate environment
  A. Plants
  B. Animals

II. Classification and its use
  A. Clarification
  B. Convenience
  C. Experimentation
     Experiment #1: Classification of plants and animals
  D. Discussion—film loop—"Lemmings"

Materials: pictures-animals, plants, collection herbariums, booklets,
    plant charts, animal charts.

Gifted Child Society
Tentative Lesson Outline

Instructor:
Course: Science for Beginners
Hour: 11:00 A.M.   Age: 6-7

Outline for 3rd week's lesson

What is a material?

  I. Familiar environmental materials

    A. Distinguish between solids, liquids, gases

    B. Critical thinking-simple generalization (cartoons)

 II. Scientific theories

    A. Molecular theory

      1. What it is

      2. How scientists use it

    B. Experimentation

    Experiment #2 Does air take up space?

    Experiment #3 Does air have weight?

Materials: magazine pictures, paste, construction paper, ice cubes,
        balloons, food coloring, balance beam, football pump

Gifted Child Society
Tentative Lesson Outline

Instructor:
Course: Science for Beginners
Hour: 11:00 A.M.   Age: 6-7

Outline for 4th week's lesson

How do heating and cooling change materials?

I. The effects of heating and cooling

A. Size changes in materials

Teacher demostration #1: Heating and cooling, change the length of wire

Demo. #2: How do heating and cooling change the volume of H_2O?

Demo. #3: How do heating and cooling change the volume of air?

B. Changes of State-Heating

Experiment #1: How does wax melt?

#2 —How does glass act when heated?

#3 — Which evaporates faster—hot H_2O or cold H_2O

Gifted Child Society
Tentative Lesson Outline

Instructor:
Course: Science for Beginners
Hour: 11:00 A.M.
Age: 6-7 years

Outline for 5th week's lesson

How can one material be changed into another?

I. Composition of material
   A. Elements
   B. Compounds
   C. Mixtures

II. Chemical Changes
   A. How is it recognized?
   B. How is it controlled?

III. Experimentation
   A. Elements
      Experiment #1: What happens when mecuric oxide is heated?
   B. Mixtures
      Experiment #2: Is soil a mixture?
   C. Recognizing chemical change
      Experiment #3: Test for starch
      Experiment #4: Acid test, base test
   D. Controlling chemical change
      Experiment #5: What effect does light have on chemical changes?

Gifted Child Society
Tentative Lesson Outline

Instructor:
Course: Science for Beginners
Hour: 11:00 A.M.
Age: 6-7 years

Outline for 6th week's lesson

How do we use and control fire?

I. Explore students' background

    A. Experience with fire

    B. Importance in their lives

    C. What is fire?

II. Meaning of oxidation

    A. Experimentation

        Tr. Experiment #1: What happens when a candle burns?

        Stu. Experiment #2: What happens when iron rusts?

III. Managing fire intelligently

    A. Material that burns

    B. Getting materials to burn

    C. Regulating fires

Materials: pictures, cartoons, chemicals

Gifted Child Society
Tentative Lesson Outline

Instructor:
Course: Science for Beginners
Hour: 11:00 A.M.
Age: 6-7 years

Outline for 7th week's lesson

How do magnets work?

I. Previous experience with magnets

A. Behavior of magnets

B. Experimentation

Experiment #1: The difference between magnetic and non-magnetic materials

Experiment #2: The force of a magnet passes through non-magnetic materials more easily than through magnetic materials

Experiment #3: Where the force of a magnet is

II. Making a magnet

A. Experimentation
Experiment #4: Magnetizing by contact
Experiment #5: Magnetizing by electric current

B. Summary and review

Gifted Child Society
Tentative Lesson Outline

Instructor:
Course: Science for Beginners
Hour: 11:00 A.M.
Age: 6-7 years

Outline for 8th week's lesson

How are all living things alike?

I. What can all animals do?
   A. Compile list of activities
   B. Energy-life forces

II. Plant life compared to animal life
   A. Experimentation
      Experiment #1: Is carbon dioxide given out in your lungs?
      Experiment #2: Does a plant give out carbon dioxide?
   B. Composition of living things
      Observation #1: What cells look like
      Observation #2: Important part of a cell

III. Composition of living things

Gifted Child Society
Tentative Lesson Outline

Instructor:
Course: Science for Beginners
Hour: 11:00 A.M.
Age: 6-7 years

Outline for 9th week's lessons

Why do you eat different kinds of food?

  I. The effect of food in the body

    A. Warmth
    B. Growth
    C. Repair

  II. Categories of foods

  III. Digestive glands of the body

  IV. Arterial part of circulatory system

  V. You are what you eat

    A. Discuss kinds of food and what they do
    B. General Mills Basic Foods chart
    C. Discussion and experimentation

Gifted Child Society
Tentative Lesson Otuline

Instructor:
Course: Science for Beginners
Hour: 11:00 A.M.
Age: 6-7 years

Outline for 10th week's lesson

How do living things depend on each other?

I. Interdependence of living things

    A. Food cycle/chain

    B. *The Sea Around Us,* Rachael L. Carson

II. Photosynthesis

    A. How green plants make food

    B. How they get materials (root systems)

    C. Observation #1: How are the roots of plants arranged?
       Experiment #1: Where are the H_2O carrying tubes of the plants?

III. Communities—plants and animals living together

Gifted Child Society
Tentative Lesson Outline

Instructor:
Course: Art for Young People
Age: 5-6 years
Hour: 11:00 A.M.

Outline for 1st week's lesson

Painting
Discuss painting and care of materials.
Test recognition of colors.
Read poem "The Clown."
Paint a picture of the clown.

Outline for 2nd week's lesson

Bird mobile
Discuss meaning of the word *mobile* and its relation to art.
Cover cardboard cones with tissue paper and acrylic.
Attach wings, beak and tail. Hang from yarn; staple to back.

Outline for 3rd week's lesson

Printing
Stress repetition and balance in composition.
Using a variety of vegetables, press on sponge with paint and print.
Choice of a variety of papers.

Outline for 4th week's lesson
Masks
Cut triangle from bogus paper. Cut out eyes, nose, and ears to
enable it to hook on head. Decorate with markers and artape. Relate
masks to various cultures.

Outline for 5th week's lesson

Puppets
Talk about types of puppets and how they work. Demonstrate stick
puppets. Cover can with cloth, decorate with trim. Attach styrofoam head to dowel; add face. Assemble.

Outline for 6th week's lesson

Nature collage
Discuss art in nature and the meaning of collage. Using background of burlap covered cardboard attach various weeds and other objects taken from nature. Stress textures.

Outline for 7th week's lesson

Clay
Explain properties of clay and demonstrate use while each one handles a piece of clay.
Make a person or animal figure. Smooth with water then texture. Add nose for next week's addition.

Outline for 8th week's lesson

Clay, continued.
Explain drying and firing process.
Paint figures, then make whimsey dip flowers or balloons to insert in holder.

Outline for 9th week's lesson

Dippity Dye
Discuss primary and secondary colors.
Demonstrate the mixing of colors.
Fold paper and dip in dyes; unfold, dry, then attach to dowel to create banner.

Outline for 10th week's lesson

Straw sculpture.
Review meaning of sculpture and balance.
Start sculpture by pushing straws into the base of plasticence.
Attach others by gluing or insertion.
Build to desired height then spray with metallic paint.

The fourth set of lesson plans is more unstructured, more informal, mainly because the course is more unstructured. The other two courses are science-oriented. Learning in the sciences is more disciplined, more dependent on the mastery of basic information, theories, and concepts. The art course does not call for the same kind of experimentation and discussion. Art is a creative experience rather than an intellectual exercise. In the first week, for example, the children will paint a picture of the character in the poem "The Clown." Children will depict the clown differently. That is the nature of art. There are no precise measurements and qualities.

Building in Flexibility

"I'm always changing strategy," says one of the Society's science teachers. "Each time I teach I find things that don't work. The teacher of gifted children has to be ready to revise—always revise."

Lesson plans are made prior to the start of the course. They identify those learning goals, objectives, activities, and materials the teacher has every reason to believe will be valid throughout the course. But they may not be valid, and that's okay. You shouldn't feel badly that you have to change learning goals midway through the course, or have to supply new or different materials, or have to design new experiments for weeks three and four because experiments in weeks one and two led to a different and more exciting area than planned.

The lesson plans also must be flexible because there will be occasions when no child will be able to finish all that has been planned according to the time schedule. There may be many times when a few children will be unable to keep up with the schedule. There will also be times when some or all of the children will move faster than you expected.

A warning also is in order. Don't allow so much flexibility and don't make so many changes that there are no longer any real learning goals for anyone. Throw away plans and activities that don't work, but do replace them with other objectives.

Ready or Not

Probably the hardest lesson for a beginning teacher of gifted children to learn is to be overprepared for a lesson and overprepared with materials. "I go in loaded for bear," says one teacher.

If you are accustomed to teaching children of all intellectual capacities, you are probably going to be unprepared for your first meeting with gifted children. Experienced teachers of gifted children find that the children use up materials and ideas and go through activities much more quickly than other children.

You may want to keep this beginning rule of thumb in mind: When you think you are ready and have everything for the day's lesson—double it.

Chapter 19

Techniques for Teaching That Really Work

Over a nineteen-year period the Gifted Child Society has offered hundreds of courses and has employed nearly as many teachers. Based on this experience, we have come up with a list of teaching/learning techniques that seem to work well with gifted children of elementary and junior high school age. The techniques are classified according to the sciences, the language, arts, and the fine arts.

In the Sciences

1. *Introduce simple devices and ideas that children can use to arrive at more complex procedures and concepts.* "You can give the gifted child a little and he will come up with a lot," says one of our science teachers. While gifted children need guidance, they don't need constant prodding. They are capable of discovering and moving from one step to another. One science teacher handed out thermometers to his students and suggested that they discover what they could about the temperature in the room. Using their thermometers, children discovered on their own such facts as these: that rising air is generally warmer and strong winds (drafts) tend to cool the air.

2. *Provide many materials for handling.* "Gifted children constantly want to get their hands wet," says another Society science teacher. There should be a lot of manipulative materials available. Most children like to feel things as well as look at them, but the gifted child tends to be more insistent on this experience and derives more from it. A teacher who wanted children to learn about the

life of early man brought in museum artifacts that people ordinarily would not be allowed to touch. But he encouraged his students to handle the artifacts so they could appreciate the difficulty of making such things by hand when most things today are machine-made.

3. *Provide many materials for construction.* Gifted children like to "get their hands wet" by putting things together. Generally, the gifted child has a longer attention span for construction than other children and learns more from the experience. In a science class studying weather, for example, children were asked to make a thermometer, a barometer, a sundial, and a weather vane.

4. *Schedule challenging experiments.* Gifted children are able to conduct and record relatively complex experiments at an early age. Children seven and eight can profit from the dissection of simple animals and insects. In a class on microbes for children who were about eight years old, the teacher had students make their own culture dishes and monitor them for growth of bacteria.

In the Language Arts

1. *Cause mental consternation.* Questions have to be phrased in a very provocative manner. This is not a simple task. The question has to be so constructed that it will encourage — force, if you will — children to open up their minds to invent, probe, and create. In the typical language arts classroom the teacher might simply ask children to describe as best they can what Robert Frost says in one of his poems or what Emily Dickinson says in one of hers. But the teacher of the gifted might say something like this: "The poetry of Robert Frost can be played on a harmonica while the works of Emily Dickinson require full orchestration. What do you suppose that means?" There are no right and wrong answers. You're pulling the cork out of a bottle and turning loose what's inside.

2. *Challenge with more than one concept or method at a time.* Gifted children generally are able to work on two or three levels at one time.

3. *Provide opportunities for the application of ideas.* Gifted children need to progress to increasingly higher levels of thinking, building each new level on the last one. If a gifted first grader has learned that two half apples make a whole one, he or she will probably quickly move along to the idea that four halves make two apples,

but that four quarters will only make one apple, that apples can be cut into sections other than halves, that a knife cannot be cut into anything so easily, and that two half ballons certainly are not as good as a whole one. Teachers: prepare!

In the Fine Arts

1. *Offer multiple experiences and activities.* It is important in the fine arts, as in the other disciplines, to provide opportunities for children to work on more than one level and engage in more than one activity. One of the Society's music teachers plays "Pictures at an Exhibition" for seven- and eight-year olds, then suggests they draw or paint some of the "pictures" or impressions described by the music. Finally, the children act out the scenes.

2. *Encourage follow-up activities.* The same teacher uses music from shows, operas, T.V., movies, and other productions that children might see at the time or in the near future. She encourages parents to buy recordings of the same music for their children. In art or sculpture classes students may be introduced to paintings and sculpture that can also be viewed at nearby museums or galleries. In order to accomplish this, the teacher must be up-to-date on what's happening in the area in the art world.

3. *Encourage individual creativity.* In the typical classroom all children may be asked to do exactly the same thing at the same time. You know how it goes: "All right, today we're going to draw a Thanksgiving turkey." In a Society workshop course called "Paint Pots, Puppets, and Prints," the art teacher had a lesson on plaster-of-paris craft in which, according to her description, "the emphasis was on individual design—utilizing the core shape as imaginatively as possible." In a sculpture class children were encouraged to form any shape they wanted with wax in a sand mold.

Chapter 20

Materials That Can Help

The materials and equipment you use depends on the subject you're teaching, the learning goals for the children, and the activities planned. But here are some tips about materials and equipment and their uses which come from the long experience of the teachers of the Gifted Child Society.

TIP 1

Be prepared to use more materials and equipment than you would for a typical class of children of the same age. We're said this before, but it bears repeating. Teachers employed by the Gifted Child Society consistently have expressed initial surprise at the amount of materials gifted children require. This is because of the gifted child's exceptional curiosity, his desire to apply what he has learned, and his ability and need to work at several different levels or with several different ideas at the same time.

TIP 2

Be prepared to supply many materials and pieces of equipment yourself. This advice is for teachers of gifted children in a program not sponsored by a public school. The Gifted Child Society has rented space in schools for its program, but the school system renting the space has not supplied either materials or equipment. In fact, the Society must remind teachers that nothing in the classroom where they are working can be moved or used, except the furniture and chalkboards. The Society does provide a minimal amount of telescopes, film and slide projectors, and phonographs. But that's about it.

Teachers of many science and art courses charge a small laboratory fee to have sufficient funds for the purchase of necessary materials and equipment. Such items would include rocket-making materials, simple dissecting tools, small animal specimens, chemicals, test tubes, culture dishes, and the various materials used for the different art forms.

However, many materials are brought in by the teacher. They include things he or she has collected at home, borrowed from museums and friends, or bought especially for the class with his or her own money. Although the Society reimburses teachers for minor expenses, some teachers prefer to donate things.

TIP 3

Be ingenious. It may be a welcome challenge to many teachers in an out-of-school program for gifted children to introduce materials that he or she would not ordinarily use in the public school. In the typical public elementary school, children draw Thanksgiving turkeys, but in an art class run by the Society, a ninety-pound teacher carted in a thirty-pound *live* turkey in a crate for the children to examine and touch. And one teacher can take advantage of the ingenuity of other teachers and their students. A language arts class exploring fables and legends might ask an art class to make hand puppets depicting the characters in the fables and legends.

TIP 4

Use materials that children can do something with—or at least touch. Don't bring in too many articles that must be marked "Do Not Touch." And don't bring in too many materials that only can be demonstrated by the teacher. If the science teacher wants to show how to make a barometer out of a glass jar, straws, glue, balloons, paper, and wood, it would be desirable for him or her to have enough of those items to go around the children in the class.

TIP 5

Use a lot of simple materials that can be turned into working parts. In a music class for gifted four- and five-year-olds the music teacher had the children make a rubber band guitar in the second lesson. A teacher in a basic physics class for children seven and eight showed them how to make a pulley and spring scale out of little plastic bottles, simple hooks and springs, and little wheels that can be bought for a couple of cents. Another teacher had children seven and eight make a working pinhole camera from oatmeal containers.

TIP 6

Supply materials children can use to make their own things. Construction plays a major role in the classroom for gifted children. This means in the sciences, language arts, fine arts, and humanities classroom. Gifted children who are seven and eight years old can build their own rockets, make their own animated film strips, and build their own simple computer. Children between ages eight and ten who are studying drama might build their own miniature theaters or their own large-scale scenery for a real production. Gifted children are ready and anxious to build things at a very early age. You have to supply the materials; the children will supply the creativity.

TIP 7

Have the students bring in materials. These might include such things as egg cartons, left-over lumber, their pets—and even a pregnant mother, for a truly rare show and tell session.

Chapter 21

Tapping the Community and Parents

The teacher in the typical public school is sometimes unable to use the resources of the community and parents to the degree he or she would like to. Not all school authorities welcome such activities. The school days are often so full that there is no time to make necessary arrangements, or the syllabus may require that so much must be done by a particular date and it is impossible to fit in extras.

Although time will always be a precious commodity, the teacher in this special program will have more of it to make advance preparations for using the resources of the community and parents. The privately-run program enables a teacher to have the freedom to do things, to utilize people and materials, and to go places otherwise not possible in the public school.

Tapping the community and parents means:

• Asking people from various occupations to visit the classroom and tell children something about their work. The Gifted Child Society has welcomed doctors, policemen, lawyers, and other career people.

• Asking people in the community and parents to bring in materials and equipment that can be demonstrated and/or used by the children. A professional photographer might bring in different kinds of cameras, lenses, and film. Some children might take a close-up picture for a color slide with one camera while other children are taking an unusual black and white picture using a fish-eye lens.

• Asking people and institutions in the community and parents to contribute materials and equipment for use in the classroom. For a lesson on banking, a local bank might contribute different kinds of forms. The town library might prepare an exhibit for your classroom. The local pharmacy might give you some empty bottles for an experiment. A parent who owns a nursery might give you cuttings from various kinds of trees and bushes.

• Asking parents to provide special services for the class. A father who works for a company that uses photocopying equipment might be willing to duplicate children's poems and essays. A mother who works in the post office might arrange to have children's art exhibited there. Parents might donate their cars and their time to drive the children somewhere.

• Going out into the community to take advantage of the resources there. The Gifted Child Society has run two very successful courses in the community: one in a hospital and the other course at a university. The "safari" that is a vital part of the Society's summer workshop takes children on week-long trips to a variety of interesting places including historical and scientific sites. Children studying astronomy visit a planetarium. Field trips should be an integral part of the course of study and not an isolated experience.

The organization you're working for should have a committee that can help you find the kinds of materials and resource persons you need. The Society's membership committee, for example, is able to tell teachers what members of the organization can offer their class the learning experience they want.

There is not a business, industry, foundation, service organization, labor union, or civic group that does not count education as a top priority. Your organization has virtually unlimited resources in terms of talented people, facilities, materials and services if it works with these groups.

Chapter 22

What You Need to Know

Salary and Working Conditions

Pay scales vary from region to region, from state to state, and even from one part of a state to another. It is not possible, therefore, to suggest a suitable salary for part-time teaching in a privately-run program for gifted children.

Earlier in this book we advocated paying a teacher in an out-of-school program for gifted children as much or, preferably, more than what is being paid teachers in other kinds of part-time educational programs operated in the area. We think this is a good rule of thumb.

We also want to repeat some advice we gave earlier. If you are looking for a way to significantly improve your income, don't consider a job teaching gifted children for an hour or two a week for perhaps twenty weeks a year. Your desire to teach gifted children in a program that permits you wide latitude in what you will teach and how you will teach it should come first. Otherwise, you probably will be disappointed. So will the children.

As a teacher you need good conditions for your instruction and the children's learning. Based on its experience, the Gifted Child Society suggests you ask these questions before signing up to teach in any such program:

1. How many children will be in my classes? The Society has kept most of its classes to between ten and sixteen children, depending

on age and subject. This permits lively discussions and allows students to work individually and in small groups.

2. How big will the classroom be? The Society always has conducted its program in rented space in either a public or a parochial school. The rooms, therefore, have always been standard classroom size. If the program you are interested in is going to be conducted in a place other than a rented school, ask if the room you will be teaching in is equivalent in size to a school room, approximately 28 by 32 feet. You can get by with something slightly smaller, but not much. Gifted children shouldn't—and usually won't—sit still in chairs at desks for an hour. They should have an opportunity to move around, to do things away from the desk. That takes space.

3. What materials and equipment will be available to me? As we have mentioned, the Gifted Child Society's teachers and children use only the furniture and chalkboards in the classrooms the Society rents. The Society does provide a minimal amount of equipment. Don't assume anything about equipment and materials. Ask. If the room you will be teaching in has no chalkboard and you will need one, you might be able to make arrangements for a portable one. Or you may have to decide to revise your classroom strategy. If there is no gas outlet in any room in the place where the educational program is being conducted and you want to use Bunsen burners, you had better know the situation in advance. You may have to make arrangements for portable burners that do not require a hook-up.

Getting Along with Your Employers

This book is all about parents of gifted children organizing to offer their children a quality, out-of-school enrichment program. If parents follow our advice, your employers will be parents. This may necessitate your rethinking your philosophy about parental involvement in the learning of their children. In a few public schools the philosophy still prevails that educators know best and that parents should be told little and listened to even less. Fortunately, this philosophy is changing in many places. The chances are that you do not resent parental involvement if you are planning to teach in a program run by parents. It's still good advice, however, to sit down and think about your philosophy before you take the job. Don't assume that because you may have worked for a board of education the experience is identical to working for an executive board of a parent organization.

Here's some advice for getting along with your employers that may help:

• Your employers started their own educational program because they felt their children weren't getting all the help they needed in the public schools. You will have to convince them that you really care about helping gifted children and that you are able to offer the children something more and different from what the public school offers.

• Remember that your salary is coming directly from parents' pockets. The relationship is much more intimate than taxpayer and public school employee. It is likely that the organization will want to evaluate your work more throughly than your public school supervisors. Getting along with your employers means expecting and cooperating with more frequent evaluations. Don't forget, there is no tenure and no appeal board.

• Make good use of members as resource persons in the classroom.

Disciplining Children

Most of the children you will be teaching *want* to be with you. The law does not require them to be there, and most parents don't force their gifted child to take a course he or she doesn't want. Also, it is unlikely that children will become frustrated and bored. If you're doing your job, the course will be geared to the unique characteristics and abilities of gifted children. You will have children for only an hour or so a week. Therefore, fewer discipline problems will arise in a small class for gifted children operated once a week than in a typical public school classroom.

If your employers are as careful as the Society, they will have asked the public schools where the children are regularly enrolled to vouch for the children's emotional maturity. But despite all precautions, you may occasionally have a child who lacks the emotional maturity or stability for the kind of learning situations you have created. In such a case you should make your employers aware of the problem as *quickly as you spot it*. Don't wait until the end of the semester— for the child's sake and yours.

Don't expect children who are seven and eight, who are operating intellectually at a very mature level, to behave like youths fourteen and fifteen. You may manufacture discipline problems if you do.

Ordinarily, minor problems such as dealing with a brief, if sometimes heated, dispute between children should be handled as it would be in any other situation where the person in charge is expected to help resolve differences fairly.

Reporting to Parents

We have discussed elsewhere in the book the Gifted Child Society's procedures for reporting in writing to parents about students' progress. A simple written report to parents similar to the one we use should be supplemented by meetings between you and parents. Reports should be honest, constructive, and tempered with mercy. Something complimentary can be said about every person, so strive to accentuate the positive about each child in your reports to parents. Often what is *not* said in a report is as important to the parent as what is said. If a teacher says the child "works best by himself," the parent will assume that the child does not do very well in group work. Any inferences drawn by parents should have been intended by the teacher. In the case cited above, it would have been been more helpful if the teacher had said the child "works well by himself but needs more encouragement and guidance in working with other children."

Some parents will not have—or will not take—the time to meet with you. For those parents who would like to personally discuss their child's work, or yours, it is desirable to arrange a meeting at a mutually convenient time. Such meetings often clear up misunderstandings parents have or give them information about the course that they don't have. Parents learn about a course and a teacher mostly from their child, but not all children are reliable reporters.

Keeping Records

The Gifted Child Society keeps a folder for each child enrolled in its program similar to the file kept for students in the public schools. You should have access to any pertinent information in the files about children enrolling in your course(s). Such information should at least include the data required at registration, such as eligibility information, any statements about the child's emotional maturity, and comments reported by previous teachers.

Expect to contribute to each child's folder your assessment of his or her work and your fair comments and observations about his or her behavior.

Afterword

Much has been written about gifted children by many fine professional people.

This book does not claim to be a professional journal; it is an accurate record of what one group of parents has learned about offering an enrichment program for their gifted children and those of many other parents. After eighteen years and 10,000 children we feel that what we have learned—possibly from a less professional viewpoint—will be valuable to other parents of gifted children and their teachers.

We have offered many do's and don'ts, guidelines and rules—all born out of practical experience and a lot of hard work.

Now we want to leave you parents and teachers with one last wish: We hope that you enjoy gifted children and what they have to offer as much as the Gifted Child Society does; our future is invested in them.

Appendix A

Gifted Child Society Constitution and By-Laws

Article I — Name

This organization shall be a non-profit organization and shall be called the Gifted Child Society, Inc.

Article II — Purpose

The purpose for which this corporation has been formed is to provide educational enrichment for intellectually gifted children and to seek public recognition of their special needs.

Article III — Membership

Membership in the Society shall be open to all persons interested in the purpose of the Society upon payment of dues as provided herein.

Article IV — Dues

Dues shall be payable annually in February for the ensuing year. The dues shall be in an amount set by the Executive Board and approved by the membership at regular meetings. In the event the amount set by the Executive Board for any year is not approved, the dues shall be the same as those last approved by the membership.

Article V — Trustees and Their Duties

A. There shall be a Board of Trustees consisting of five members who shall be elected as trustees by the members of the Society as provided in Article X hereof. Said trustees shall be elected at each annual meeting and shall hold office until the next annual meeting and until successor trustees shall have been elected and qualified.

B. The Board of Trustees shall establish and be responsible for the execution of its policies and shall supervise the activities of the Executive Board in order that the objectives and purposes of this Society may be fulfilled.

C. The Board of Trustees shall meet at least once a year at the annual meeting of the Society to appoint the president.

D. Three members of the Board of Trustees shall constitute a quorum for the transaction of business. No voting by proxy shall be permitted.

E. At the first meeting of the Board of Trustees after its election, the Board shall elect a chairman and a secretary to conduct the Board's business for the term of its election.

F. The Board of Trustees may appoint one of its members as president of the Society.

G. Any vacancy on the Board of Trustees shall be filled by an election by the Executive Board of the Society, and said trustee elected thereby shall serve out the remainder of the term left vacant.

Article VI — Officers

I. Officers: The officers of this Society shall be president, first vice president, second vice president, recording secretary, corresponding secretary and treasurer. Said officers, except the president, shall be appointed at the annual meeting by the president.

A. Presidential Qualifications:

  1. The president of the Society shall meet one of the following qualifications:

    a. He shall be a superintendent of schools or
    b. He shall be a president of a college or university or
    c. He shall be a public figure who by the nature of his stature and accomplishments would serve the interests of this Society in the furtherance of its purposes.

  2. In the event the Board of Trustees is unable or fails to appoint a president of this Society at the time of the an-

nual meeting, then the Board of Trustees shall appoint a first vice president to assume the duties of the president until a president is appointed. The first vice president appointed at said annual meeting shall assume the duties of the president until such time as a president is appointed. At said annual meeting, a special committee shall be appointed by the Board of Trustees for the purpose of seeking a qualified person or persons who shall be suitable for the office of president and whose name it shall submit to the Board of Trustees.

B. Duties of the Officers

1. President:

   a. The president shall preside at all meetings of the Society and at all Executive Board meetings.

   b. He shall be ex-officio member of all committees, except the nominating committee referred to in Article X hereof.

   c. He shall countersign all checks, signed by the treasurer and approved by the Executive Board or as provided in the budget.

   d. He shall appoint the chairmen of all the committees, both standing and special.

   e. He shall, with the consent of the Executive Board, remove committee chairmen.

   f. He shall perform all the other duties pertaining to the office, and entrusted to him by the Board of Trustees, in order that the objectives and purposes of this Society may be fulfilled.

2. First Vice President:

   a. He shall assume the duties of the president, in the absence of or at the request of the president.

   b. He shall perform those functions which the president shall direct.

3. Second Vice President:

   a. He shall assume the duties of the president in the absence of the president and first vice president or at the request of the president or acting president.

b. He shall perform those functions which the president shall direct.

4. Recording Secretary:

He shall record the minutes of all regular and Executive Board meetings of the Society and perform such other duties as may be directed by the president or the Executive Board.

5. Corresponding Secretary:

a. Send or cause to be sent, to all members, the proper notice of all membership meetings.
b. Send or cause to be sent, to all members of the Executive Board, proper notice of all Executive Board meetings.
c. He shall perform all other functions as directed by the president or the Executive Board.

6. Treasurer:

a. He shall receive and deposit all monies of the Society.
b. He shall disburse such sums as provided by the budget or as voted by the Executive Board or the membership.
c. He shall keep an accurate record of receipts and expenditures.
d. He shall present a brief financial statement at every regular meeting of the membership and also at Executive Board meetings if requested.
e. He shall make a detailed financial report at the annual meeting.
f. He shall perform all other functions as directed by the president.

Article VII — Executive Board

I. Duties:

A. Except as otherwise provided in this Constitution, the Executive Board shall have the power to transact the business of the Society.

B. The Executive Board shall consist of the president, the first vice president, the second vice president, the recording secretary, the corresponding secretary, the treasurer and the chairman of the standing committees.

C. Each officer and each committee chairman shall have one vote on any one issue.

D. There shall be no voting by proxy.

E. In the event that there is a vice-chairman of a standing committee, only the chairman has the right to vote. In the absence of the chairman, the vice-chairman shall have the right to vote.

F. In no case shall any one member have more than one vote on any one issue.

G. Budget:

1. The Executive Board shall present to the membership for its approval an annual budget for the period February 1 through the following January 31. This budget shall be presented at the November or December meeting prior to the budget.

2. In the event the budget is not approved at this meeting, the Executive Board shall proceed forthwith to present an acceptable budget.

H. In the event a budget is presented to the membership and approved, no other monies may be spent by the Executive Board, except with the approval of the membership.

I. In the event a budget is not approved by the membership, the Executive Board shall have the authority to spend not in excess of $1,000.00 per month without the approval of the membership.

J. In the event that a committee chairman has been absent for three consecutive Executive Board meetings, the president shall, with the approval of the Executive Board, replace him with another chairman.

K. The Executive Board shall meet once every month unless otherwise voted by the Board.

L. A quorum for this Executive Board shall consist of more than half its active members.

M. The Executive Board shall arrange for an annual audit of the books of the treasurer.

Article VII — Standing Committees

I. The standing committees shall be as provided herein:

Community Action	Planning and Finance
Curriculum	Program
Hospitality	Publicity
Information Clearinghouse	Research
Legislative Action	Saturday Workshop Activities
Library	Scholarship
Membership Participation	Ways and Means
Newsletter	

II.

A. The chairmen of the standing committees shall be appointed by the president each year after his appointment and before the next regular meeting.

B. The chairmen of the standing committees shall present general plans of work to the Executive Board for approval. No action shall be taken until the general plans are approved. Upon approval of such plans, the committee shall take charge of and execute them. The committee shall execute other instructions that may be given it by the Executive Board.

Article IX — Meetings

I. Dates:

A. Regular meetings of this Society shall be held at least three times a year, unless otherwise provided by the membership of the Executive Board.

B. In the event a meeting date is changed, at least ten days notice of said new meeting date must be given to the membership.

C. A special membership meeting may be called by the Executive Board with at least ten days notice being given to the membership.

II. Miscellaneous:

A. A quorum shall consist of a least fifteen percent of the total membership or twenty members in good standing, whichever is smaller.

B. A member in good standing is a member whose dues for the current year are paid.

C. Voting Member: For the purposes of voting at a regular meeting, the husband and wife of the member family in good standing shall each have one vote.

D. The regular meeting in November or December shall be known as the annual meeting and shall be for the purpose of electing trustees, receiving reports of officers and committees, and for any other business that may arise.

Article X — Elections and Terms of Office

I. Nominations:

A. Nominating Committee: A nominating committee of five members shall be appointed annually in the first quarter of the year by the Executive Board. The nominating committee shall prepare a slate of trustees to be presented at the regular meeting of the Society prior to the annual meeting and at the annual meeting.

B. Nominations will be accepted from the floor at both these meetings.

C. The corresponding secretary shall notify the membership of the slate of proposed trustees before the regular meeting prior to the annual meeting.

D. Members of the nominating committee may be nominated for trustees.

II. All trustees and officers shall serve for one year from annual meeting to annual metting and until their successors shall have been elected and appointed. They may be re-elected and re-appointed to serve consecutive terms.

Article XI — Vacancies in Office

I. In the event that a vacancy arises in any office other than that of the president, that vacancy shall be filled by the Executive Board.

II. In the event that there is a vacancy in the office of the president, those provisions applying to the appointment of president shall be followed. [See Article VI]

Article XII — Amendments

I. This Constitution and By-laws may be amended by a two-thirds vote of the members voting, a quorum being present, provided that this amendment has been presented in writing to every member in good standing at least ten days before the meeting at which the vote is to be taken.

II. When a motion to amend is properly before the membership, it shall be the duty of the corresponding secretary to provide the notice in writing to the members.

III. In order to properly place a motion to amend this Constitution before the membership, the following steps must be taken:

   A. A motion must be made at a regular meeting.

   B. This motion must be approved by nine other members in good standing.

   C. This motion and the approval of the nine other members must be presented to the recording secretary.

   D. This motion shall then be tabled until the next regular meeting or until a special meeting for its consideration shall be called. At this meeting, proper notice having been given, it shall be read, discussed and voted upon.

Article XIII — Rules of Order

Roberts' Rules of Order, as most recently revised, shall be the authority for procedures in all cases in which they are applicable, and in which they are not inconsistent with these By-laws.

Appendix B

Job Descriptions for Positions of Executive Director, School Coordinator, and Curriculum Coordinator

The Executive Director

Appointment:

The executive director is appointed by the Executive Board, but he/she is not a member of it.

The position is paid, and it is subject to re-appointment at the end of each calendar year.

Responsibilities:

The executive director is responsible for the efficient and harmonious functioning of all aspects of the Society. He/she assists committee chairmen in obtaining the goals of their committees and is ultimately responsible for the Society's educational programs, brochures, newsletters and membership meetings.

The executive director acts as the administrative assistant to the president and facilitates his duties whenever possible.

The executive director acts as liaison between the president and the Executive Board, Society employees, special committee chairmen and the membership at large.

The executive director represents the Society to all outside agencies and individuals. He/she acts as consultant and information clearinghouse to education agencies, legislators and the public at large. He/she is available in person, through the mails, on the telephone and at the Society's educational programs to all groups and individuals supporting education for the gifted.

181

The executive director is responsible for the business of the Society being conducted in accordance with its constitution.

Philosophy:

The Executive Director fulfills his/her duties in a spirit of co-opration and service and devotes himself/herself to maintaining rapport with all his/her contacts.

The School Coordinator

Appointment:

The school coordinator is appointed by the Executive Board, but he/she is not a voting member of this board. The appointment is subject to confirmation before each registration period. It is a full-time job during registration periods. It is paid at the end of each registration period.

Responsibilities:

The school coordinator is responsible for the registration and maintenance of the Society's Workshop programs within established procedures.

The school coordinator cooperates with all committee chairmen whose work is connected with Workshop programs.

The school coordinator is aware of and carries out the policies and directions of the Executive Board at all times.

The school coordinator holds in safekeeping the supplies and equipment necessary to fulfill his/her duties.

Limitations:

The school coordinator seeks the guidance of the school committee in all matters not covered by established procedures, and in his/her contacts with parents outside the routine mechanics of registration and maintenance of the Workshop programs.

The school coordinator refers all matters regarding curriculum and teacher supervision to the curriculum coordinator and/or the curriculum committee.

The School Coordinator passes all other new business to the Executive Board and/or the Executive Secretary without action.

Philosophy:

The school coordinator fulfills his/her duties in the spirit of cooperation and service, and he/she devotes himself/herself to maintaining rapport with all his/her contacts.

The Coordinator of Curriculum and Instruction

Appointment

The coordinator of curriculum and instruction is appointed by the Executive Board, but he/she is not a voting member of it.

The position is salaried, and it is subject to re-appointment before each registration period.

General Responsibilities

The coordinator is responsible for curriculum development and for the improvement of instruction in the fall and spring semesters of the Saturday Workshops.

The coordination of the overall program is to be executed with the cooperation and suggestions of the curriculum committee, the Executive Board, teachers and student council.

The coordinator is to put into action the cooperatively planned educational program appropriate to the goals of the Society.

The coordinator is responsible for preparing, with the cooperation of individual teachers, the course descriptions for each semester's brochure. In addition, a course index and teacher's profile is to be prepared for the brochure.

The coordinator will be available each Saturday the Workshop is in session.

Specific Responsibilities

Curriculum: The coordinator is to recommend curriculum programs to the Executive Board and advise it of their merits.

The coordinator is to prepare a schedule for all courses offered.

The coordinator is to schedule meetings with the curriculum committee, the executive secretary and the school coordinator, with a report prepared to be presented at monthly Executive Board meetings.

Teachers: The coordinator is to make recommendations for the hiring and firing of teacher personnel.

A major responsibility is to observe instruction and prepare observation reports with the assistance of the curriculum committee.

The coordinator is responsible for assisting in the orientation of new teachers.

The coordinator is responsible for assisting in the orientation and/or soliciting references of new teachers.

The coordinator, when called for, is to act as liaison between parents and teachers, and between teachers and the Executive Board. Extraordinary complications will be referred to the Executive Board.

Appendix C

Letter and Questionnaire to a Superintendent of Schools

Dear Superintendent:

While the State of New Jersey is a recognized national leader in the education of handicapped children, only recently have school leaders focused their attention on the thousands of children who possess exceptional academic and artistic talents. At the present time, the State Department of Education is developing a master plan for the gifted and talented, and proposed legislation is presently being reviewed by the State Assembly's Committee on Education.

Notwithstanding these commendable centralized efforts, we believe that a number of school districts throughout the state have already developed, or are interested in developing, instructional programs for children whose intellectual talents outreach their chronological age.

This questionnaire, developed by the Gifted Child Society, and sanctioned by the Bergen County Department of Superintendents, has two objectives — obtaining the views of selected school superintendents and the procurement of information on existing programs to be compiled into a handbook.

Your assistance would be greatly appreciated.

GINA GINSBERG, Executive Director
Gifted Child Society, Inc.

The Gifted Child Society, Inc.

59 Glen Gray Road
Oakland, N.J.

Board Philosophy

Our school district's philosophy, as adopted by the Board of Education, can be best described by the statement: (Please check one)

.... A distinction *is not made* between the objectives of general education and those that relate to the education of the gifted and talented child.

.... A distinction *is made* between the objectives of general education and those that relate to the education of the gifted and talented child.

Student Grouping

Which of the following best describes the manner in which your district's elementary schools organize children for the instruction of reading and mathematics: (Please check one)

.... Complete heterogeneous grouping, with little or no emphasis on a child's achievement and ability.

.... Modified heterogeneous grouping in which the teachers in the same grade level organize youngsters according to their achievement and ability.

.... The achievement and ability of children are considered prime factors in grouping youngsters for reading and mathematics instruction.

Curriculum

In our elementary schools, if a third grade child successfully completes the traditional third grade work in arithmetic in March, which of the following usually occurs: (Please check one)

.... The student reviews all previous work to insure further mastery of the subject matter.

.... The student is assigned additional work and given new materials within the structure of third grade arithmetic.

.... The student is guided into fourth grade arithmetic.

.... None of the above.

In which grade level are students grouped into honors classes?

.... Primary (K - 3)

.... Upper Elementary (4 - 5)

.... Middle Grades (6 - 7 - 8)

.... Grades 9 - 10

.... Grades 11 - 12

.... We do not have "honors" classes

Appendix D

The Saturday Workshops
Sponsored by the Gifted Child Society, Inc.

Dear Instructor:

Enclosed please find:

1. Our teacher guidelines for your information.

2. Our curriculum forms with instruction letter.

3. Our reimbursement request form.

4. Stamped self-addressed envelope.

Please complete the curriculum forms and send them to our curriculum coordinator.

Please use the reimbursement request form to claim your workshop expenses. This form should be submitted with itemized receipts by the end of the semester.

Thank you for your cooperation.

Best wishes for a successful semester.

The Saturday Workshops

Sponsored by the Gifted Child Society, Inc.

To Our Teaching Staff

We have seven teenage assistants. If you need assistance in your class or classes every Saturday, please advise the school coordinator. If you expect to need help only occasionally, please request an assistant the preceding Saturday.

Discrepancies in class lists *MUST* be reported to the school coordinator the first day of school.

Absence and lateness forms (available at the desk) *MUST* be left with the school coordinator on the same date the *second* lateness or absence occurs.

Teachers must provide suitable substitutes when unable to teach, and the curriculum coordinator must be advised in advance.

Teachers are required to prepare duplicate evaluation reports for each student.

Teachers are required to sign an attendance sheet before class time when entering the building.

The Saturday Workshop owns: two record players, one tape recorder, one movie projector, one film strip projector, one overhead projector, five microscopes, and five portable safety burners. Teachers must leave their reservations for these aids with one week ahead of time.

School will be closed Easter weekend.

189

Receipted bill for materials, etc., must be submitted with the attached reimbursement request form to the school coordinator in one package at the end of the semester. Teachers will be reimbursed after completion of the semester together with their salary check. Supply houses may bill the Gifted Child Society direct to for supplies in excess of fifty dollars.

Instructors are requested to dismiss classes five minutes before the next class.

Teacher are requested to use the parking lot.

Best wishes for a successful semester!

THE SCHOOL COMMITTEE

The Saturday Workshops

Sponsored by the Gifted Child Society, Inc.

To Our Teaching Staff

We have seven teenage assistants. If you need assistance in your class or classes every Saturday, please advise the school coordinator. If you expect to need help only occasionally, please request an assistant the preceding Saturday.

Discrepancies in class lists *MUST* be reported to the school coordinator the first day of school.

Absence and lateness forms (available at the desk) *MUST* be left with the school coordinator on the same date the *second* lateness or absence occurs.

Teachers must provide suitable substitutes when unable to teach, and the curriculum coordinator, must be advised in advance. Make certain your substitute completes a "Substitute Form." The G.C.S. will pay all substitute teachers—*do not* pay the substitute teacher yourself.

Teachers are required to prepare duplicate evaluation reports for each student. All faculty obligations must be met prior to receipt of salary checks.

Teachers are required to sign an attendance sheet before class time when entering the building. A teacher check-in list is located at the school coordinator's desk. Teachers should plan to be at their rooms *at least* ten minutes before their class is scheduled to begin. Please end your class at the appropriate time (ten minutes before the hour) since other students and teachers may be scheduled to use your room and need these few minutes for preparation.

Members of the observation committee will observe class from time to time and will wear an identification tag indicating their name and position. All members of the observation committee are also members of the Executive Board of the Gifted Child Society, Inc., (please refer to the enclosure regarding the observation committee).

The Saturday Workshop presently owns two record players, one tape recorder, one movie projector, one filmstrip projector, one overhead projector, five microscopes, and five portable safety burners. Teachers must leave their reservations for these aids with the school coordinator one week ahead.

Receipted bills for materials, etc., must be submitted with the attached reimbursement request form to the school coordinator, in one package at the end of the semester. Teachers will be reimbursed after completion of the semester. Supply houses may bill the Gifted Child Society, Inc., direct for supplies in excess of fifty dollars.

Teachers are requested to use the parking lot. Street parking is not permitted. PLEASE BE CAREFUL OF CHILDREN WHEN DRIVING THROUGH THE PARKING LOT.

Best wishes for a successful semester!

Curriculum Coordinator/
Teacher Supervisor

School Coordinator

The Saturday Workshops

Sponsored by the Gifted Child Society, Inc.

———

REIMBURSEMENT REQUEST

The amount shown below was expended on behalf of the Gifted Child Society.

My itemized receipt is attached.

Name of claimant...

Address of claimant..

Amount...

Nature of expenditure...

Date...

Approved...

Date...

GIFTED CHILD SOCIETY
Tentative Lesson Outline

Instructor ....

Course ....

Age Group ....

Hour ....

Outline for........week's lesson

GIFTED CHILD SOCIETY
Tentative Lesson Outline

Instructor ....

Course ....

Age Group ....

Hour ....

Outline for........week's lesson

GIFTED CHILD SOCIETY
Tentative Lesson Outline

Instructor ....

Course ....

Age Group ....

Hour ....

Outline for........week's lesson

GIFTED CHILD SOCIETY
Tentative Lesson Outline

Instructor ....

Course ....

Age Group ....

Hour ....

Outline for........week's lesson

* Be sure to make a copy for yourself!

Appendix E

A Typical Advertisement

- MINI-SCIENTIST
- MODEL ROCKETRY
- COMPUTERS
- TIC TAC TYPING
- MINI-MUSIC MAKERS
- SCIENCE SMORGASBORD
- AMERICAN HERITAGE
- PAINT POTS and PIZZAZZ
- STAR TREK
- NUMBERAMA

These and many more exciting courses for your

Bright and Gifted Children

aged four through teens

The Saturday Workshop

at the Benjamin Franklin Jr. High School
Ridgewood, N.J.
(sponsored by the non-profit Gifted Child Society, Inc.)
For FREE spring brochure write School Coordinator
469 Churchill Road, Teaneck, N.J. 07666
or phone 837-3950

Appendix F

A Letter in Support of Bill S-874

I am offering this testimony both as the executive director of the Gifted Child Society in New Jersey, a non-profit parent organization, and as the mother of two gifted children.

The Gifted Child Society has offered educational enrichment for gifted children on Saturdays and during the summer for the past sixteen years.

During this time, the Society has provided stimulating and exciting programs for almost 10,000 students. These children joyfully and enthusiastically participate in our Saturday and summer programs, yet in their regular classrooms many of them are unrecognized, unchallenged, underachieving, or acting out their boredom and frustration to the detriment of themselves and their classmates.

We strongly support Bill S-874 by offering our sixteen years of experience in programming and teacher training for gifted children.

We applaud the establishment of a *National Clearinghouse on Gifted and Talented Children,* since our organization during the past twelve months alone has responded to almost 2,000 requests for information on gifted children. Our films and statistics, together with our recorded experiences on how to organize and operate educational programs for our gifted children, are at the disposal of this Clearinghouse.

Our children desperately need *programs for gifted and talented students through the high-school level.* It is the ultimate aim of the

Gifted Child Society to work toward its own demise, and to free its students on Saturdays and during the summer, by having the public schools provide the kind of education which will encourage them to learn as much as they are able to learn for personal fulfillment and to benefit all mankind.

We are only too aware of the importance of special *training of personnel for the gifted and talented*. Our own State of New Jersey does not train such teachers now. The Gifted Child Society would be happy to share what it has learned about desirable training, talents and characteristics for personnel for the gifted.

We wholeheartedly support *research and demonstration projects for the education of gifted and talented children*. Our records, the talents and efforts of our research committee, and our ongoing educational programs are at the disposal of the National Institute of Education. On February 28th of this year, we submitted to the Institute a proposal to research our own history to determine a formula by which similar successful programs might be started elsewhere.

The Darwinian theory of the survival of the fittest is contradicted by our current system of education which often does not even recognize its fittest and most able students, let alone help them do their best. This waste of brainpower and talent surely is the most shocking waste in our conservation conscious age!

We accept the fact that handicapped children, for instance, need different educational programs and special teachers. Gifted children, too, have special needs which must be met to enable them to fulfill their potential and take their rightful place in Society.

For the sake of our children today, and for a better life for all tomorrow, we implore the Committee to accept Bill S-874 and return it to the Senate with recommendations for passage.

GINA GINSBERG, Executive Director
Gifted Child Society, Inc.

9810